*"Time by
Moments
Steals Away"*

"Time by Moments Steals Away"

The 1848 Journal of Ruth Douglass

Robert L. Root, Jr.

 WAYNE STATE UNIVERSITY PRESS   DETROIT

Great Lakes Books
A complete listing of the books in this series can be found at the back of
this volume.

PHILIP P. MASON, *Editor*
Department of History, Wayne State University

DR. CHARLES K. HYDE, *Associate Editor*
Department of History, Wayne State University

02 01 00 99 98   5 4 3 2 1

Library of Congress Cataloging-in-Publication Data

Root, Robert L.
  Time by moments steals away : the 1848 journal of Ruth Douglass. Robert L. Root, Jr.
    p. cm. — (Great Lakes books)
  Includes bibliographical references and index.
  ISBN 0-8143-2813-x (alk. paper)
    1. Women pioneers—Middle West—Diaries. 2. Women pioneers—Isle
Royale (Mich.)—Diaries.   3. Douglass, Ruth, 1824–1850—Diaries.
4. Frontier and pioneer life—Middle West.   5. Frontier and pioneer
life—Isle Royale (Mich.)   6. Middle West—Biography.   7. Isle
Royale (Mich.)—Biography.   I. Douglass, Ruth, 1824–1850.
II. Title. III. Series.
CT275.D867R66   1998   98-6201
977.4'99703'092—dc21
[B]

Grateful acknowledgment is
made to the Mary Dickey
Masterton Fund for financial
assistance in the publication of
this volume.

For MARIE LINDERMAN ROOT, *my mother,*
and ANNA BUDNACK LINDERMAN, *my grandmother,*
from whom I learned about loss and memory

It is an absorbing thing to watch the process of world-making;—both the formation of the natural and the conventional world. I witnessed both in America; and when I look back upon it now, it seems as if I had been in another planet.

HARRIET MARTINEAU, *Society in America*

Critical acumen is exerted in vain to uncover the past; the *past* cannot be *presented*; we cannot know what we are not. But one veil hangs over past, present, and future, and it is the province of the historian to find out, not what was, but what is. Where a battle has been fought, you will find nothing but the bones of men and beasts; where a battle is being fought, there are hearts beating. We will sit on a mound and muse, and not try to make these skeletons stand on their legs again. Does nature remember, think you, that they *were* men, or not rather that they *are* bones?

THOREAU, *A Week on the Concord and Merrimack Rivers*

Contents

Acknowledgments   *11*

A Note on the Text   *13*

Introduction   *15*

The Journal of Ruth Edgerton Douglass   53

Epilogue   *113*

Appendix A. Douglass Family Genealogy   *120*

Appendix B. Newberry Family Genealogy   *121*

Appendix C. Smith Family   *122*

Bibliography   *123*

Index   *131*

Acknowledgments

Archives are fascinating and surprising places to work, treasure houses of obscure and unique information. They are happy places to work for those who enjoy the thrill of detection, the jolt of discovery, the intimacy of working with rare manuscripts and personal documents. On this book I have been aided on-site, by correspondence, and by a host of archivists and librarians around the Midwest. I have especially appreciated the assistance of Evelyn Leasher and archivist Craig G. Wright at the Clarke Historical Library at Central Michigan University, as well as Ann Sindelmeyer at Western Reserve Historical Society, Case Western Reserve University. I also wish to thank Anne Frantilla at the Bentley Historical Library, University of Michigan; Theresa Spence and Eric Nordberg at the Michigan Technological University Archives; Karen Weston at the University of Wisconsin-Whitewater; Alice E. Paquette at the Houghton County (Michigan) Historical Society; Mary King at the Madison County (New York) Historical Society; Richard F. Brown at the Waterville (New York) Historical Society; Linda Stanley at the Historical Society of Pennsylvania; and the staffs of the Library of Michigan, the Burton Collection at the Detroit Public Library, and the State of Wisconsin Historical Society. I must also thank David Langenberg, University of Delaware, a descendant of Aurilla Douglass Atwood, and Lloyd Tucker Wescoat, great-great-granddaughter of Columbus C. Douglass for sharing information on the Douglass family. The editorial board of Wayne State University Press provided guidance in adherence to historical research norms in documentation, coverage, and tone; I must take responsibility for any factual errors and residual compassion toward the subject. I am grateful to my wife, Susan Root, for sharing my travels in search of Ruth Douglass and, for their encouragement, our children, Caroline Root, Tom Root, and especially Becky Wildfong, whose summer on Isle Royale was the catalyst for my pursuing this project to its completion.

Permissions to reproduce photographs and manuscripts have been provided by the Clarke Historical Library, Central Michigan University, for publication of the journal of Mrs. C. C. Douglass and the facsimile of the final entry in the journal; by the Bentley Historical Library, University of Michigan, for the drawing of C. C. Douglass by Bela Hubbard (Hubbard Papers), the 1849 lithograph of Cliff Mine, the lithograph of Columnar Trap [Scovill Point], Isle Royale, from Foster and Whitney, the 1848 geological map of Isle Royale, the section map of Isle Royale by William Ives, and the 1868 photograph of the Surviving Siskowit Mine Building; by the State Historical Society of Wisconsin for the portrait of Christopher Douglass and the drawing of C. L. Douglass's farm in Wisconsin; by the Western Reserve Historical Society for the illustration of Leander Ransom's 1847 additions to John Locke's 1843 map of Isle Royale and Ohio holdings on Isle Royale, the facsimile of a share of Isle Royale and Ohio Mining Company stock held by Elisha Whittlesey, and permission to quote from Leander Ransom's letter to Elisha Whittlesey; by the Burton Historical Collection, Detroit Public Library, for the illustration of the Douglass Houghton Mine location; and by Lloyd Tucker Wescoat, for the photographs of Columbus, Lydia, Courtney, and Katharine Douglass.

A Note on the Text

The book that C. C. Douglass gave to Ruth Douglass on January 1, 1848, was a seven by twelve-and-a-half-inch bound volume, *The Daily Journal for 1848*, published by Francis and Loutrel, Manufacturing Stationers in New York. The journal divided each page into three equal portions, two pages per week. Because it was a business journal rather than a diary it included no spaces for Sundays, which is why the final entry is on Saturday, December 30. Except for February 22–24, when she used up three portions to write her account of her father-in-law's life history, Ruth used only one space per entry, and frequently left entries blank.

The Clarke Historical Library received a typescript of the journal accompanying their autograph copy, which I used as the initial basis of my own transcription. I retyped a photocopy of the typescript and compared the printout of that transcript with the photocopy of the complete journal and, on at least three separate occasions, against the original manuscript itself. In publishing my corrected transcription, I have tried to reproduce the spelling and punctuation of the journal as accurately as possible. In the few places where Ruth Douglass inserted a word or phrase after having completed the line or crossed out a letter or word and continued writing, I have accounted for her editing in the transcription. Her insertions and strikethroughs are infrequent. Except in a few cases where I have inserted a letter that has been omitted in the manuscript by inadvertence rather than choice (as in "fa[r]ther," "yiel[d]ing," and "beginni[n]g"), I have added no corrections or silent emendations, even in cases where her intended meaning is clearly something different from what she wrote (as when she writes the word "comfortable" instead of the word "comforter").

It may be argued that my transcription is not fully accurate—indeed, I would be one of those who would make the argument—but I doubt whether we will ever be able to be fully accurate because of two habits of Ruth Douglass's orthography. I have found only one word in the manu-

13

script that I am unable to decipher—the last name of a woman whose death was reported to Ruth in a letter from her sister and mother—but I have been continually frustrated by Ruth's inconsistent use of lowercase and uppercase letters at the start of sentences, clauses, and sentence fragments. The voice of the journal keeper generally allows omission and elision of sentence subjects, particularly pronouns, and encourages starting sentences with unagented verbs. It also encourages adding afterthoughts to completed sentences and statements as if they had not been completed. Very often the capitalization and punctuation give no certainty as to the author's consciousness of her syntax, especially when the marks we usually would take to be commas or periods are made in places we would not expect to use them or, more often, when the mark itself is too long for a period or too blunt for a comma and neither visual identification nor standard syntax can be relied upon to resolve the confusion.

Because it is important here to give the reader a sense of what it is like to read Ruth Douglass's journal the way a reader of the original manuscript encounters it, I have preferred to let these confusions stand rather than silently modernize and regularize the punctuation. Her meaning is usually clear enough that standardizing her mechanics is not necessary for understanding and might actually impose limits on her meaning. More troubling, it would interfere with the reader's clear reception of the voice that rises off the page of the manuscript. For these reasons, none of the transcription has silently emended or corrected Ruth Douglass's manuscript, although in the matter of punctuation and capitalization, we may never be able to determine fully where the transcription has been flatly wrong.

Introduction

Only a few occasions in the life of Ruth Edgerton Douglass are preserved in public records. From them we know that she was born in Sangerfield, New York, on September 30, 1824, the daughter of Isaac H. Edgerton and Louisa Newberry; that she was married to Columbus C. Douglass in Detroit, Michigan, on August 27, 1847; that not long after the birth of her only child she died in Ontonagon, Michigan, on June 11, 1850. She is recorded in some histories of the Newberry family, with sparse or erroneous information, but is never noted in the obituaries, capsule biographies, or genealogical entries about her husband. Beyond these public records she is merely mentioned in a note and a letter existing in Douglass family archives and in the journal of a Methodist missionary who, the day after her death, visited the building where her body lay. Two monuments in Detroit's Elmwood Cemetery preserve her memory, one a white obelisk engraved with her name and that of her son (her husband is buried elsewhere) and the other a memorial to the Edgerton family.

These records are of the sort that the majority of us are sure to leave behind, but they say virtually nothing about who Ruth Douglass was. Only one item provides any clues to her personality and her life—the artifact that has been the starting place for this book, the journal of Mrs. C. C. Douglass for a single year, 1848. Since its purchase by the Clarke Historical Library at Central Michigan University, it has been consulted for information about the life of a mining superintendent's wife on Isle Royale and cited numerous times by mining, Isle Royale, and Upper Peninsula scholars. We have only a handful of firsthand accounts of life on Isle Royale during the first period of the copper boom, and the journal is valuable for the fullness of the picture it paints of the period and the place.

But for anyone who has read the entire journal, the most haunting element is the lively but unfinished portrait of the woman who wrote it. A reluctant writer much of the time, she claimed at the outset of her "journal of our migrations" that she would "not attempt to carry out the design of the author" by recording her days thoroughly and faithfully but rather would "endeavor to record incidents as they may occur." The entries were made irregularly throughout the year, and sometimes whole weeks and even a month could pass without her writing a single entry.

Yet from the very first lines, when she memorably phrases her intentions and takes charge of the book, she gives the reader a sense of who she is. The first dated entry for New Year's Day suggests a quiet humor—"I think it is becoming fashionable to have wet New Year's"—and a genteel faith in the power of poetry to express profound feelings. Her gentility speaks through her reserved response to adversity, as when she observes on January 14, after an arduous journey, "about tired of stage riding in Winter, and quite happy to get to our journey's end." By the time, months later (September 8), that she records having slipped off a rock into the frigid waters around Isle Royale with the remark, "This was my first bath in Lake Superior," we can imagine the wry and reassuring comments she must have made while her husband hurriedly rowed her across Rock Harbor to a fire and dry clothing. Her reserve barely betrays her distress when her husband informs her that he has been asked to superintend a mine on Isle Royale through the coming winter. When he asks her to come with him, she answers cheerily, but lets herself hint in her journal about her reluctance. On their arrival at Isle Royale she observes acidly that the sight of it "was anything but a favorable one for me at least . . . as my eyes had not the gift of magnifying every little seam in the rocks into a large vein of Copper" (August 30).

Ruth Douglass evinces not only reserve but also resiliency. Shortly after her arrival she records an approving description of the superintendent's house ("very large and quite convenient, having eight large rooms on the first floor, also commodious chambers" [August 31]) and yard ("very neatly laid out, with graveled walks, and railings, dividing the garden into squares and beds" [September 1]). She finds humor in a "guide board to direct the wandering traveler through this densely populated city" (September 5) and the way the weather "affects business matters . . . in this small city" (October 3). Unlike her husband, busied with the superintendency of the Isle Royale & Ohio Company mines, whose locations he visits almost daily, she is frequently confined by weather to the house or has her days circumscribed by the settlement ("have been to the Engine House only twice to day" [October 7]). She is diverted by the visits of mining officials, occasional tourists, miners arriving or leaving the island or procuring provisions for more remote locations; occasionally she has the company of another agent's wife.

Much of her time is spent in small matters: caring for a puppy, reading newly published novels and biographies of historical figures, preserving quinces sent from Detroit, and making comforters for the coming winter. She writes letters, hopes for news from home, rereads old letters when no new ones arrive, and notes how the community energizes with the arrival of a vessel.

Evident beneath the surface of her letters is her anxiety over the winter to come. Columbus himself had set her anxiety in motion by telling her the day he informed her of the job offer that "he had led something of a back woods life, and was ready to go to almost any place, but the thought of being banished to a desolate island was something that had not entered his head" (August 1). On isolated Isle Royale the company town of Ransom lost population with the lateness of the season, the worsening of weather, and the imminent closing of shipping and passenger service. Some miners' wives came only for the summer; they retreated, with or without their husbands, to civilization for the remainder of the year. The mining crews themselves were reduced seasonally. Visitors stopped arriving on tours of Lake Superior. Experienced island hands guessed when the harbor would freeze and the last vessel of the season would get through, and visitors whose departures were delayed by inclement weather and the unpredictability of a vessel's arrival heightened Ruth's anxiety with their frantic fears of being trapped on the island for the winter.

Her own fears were increased by her husband's almost daily absences. The mining sites he superintended were scattered around the island, and most of the time he set out to visit them in an open boat, leaving the protection of the harbor for the often turbulent lake, rounding a rocky shoreline with only occasional harbors and frequently forbidding landfalls. Often Ruth was uncertain of his safety until he returned, much later than expected, having been forced to tie up the boat against overpowering headwinds and hike home or, on one occasion, to struggle against hypothermia after falling through the harbor ice. Much of the time Ruth must have felt as though she had been banished, exiled.

Such a moment occurs in her journal entry for November 2, after she takes "a walk up the steep rocky ridge which rises nearly one hundred feet just back of our residence." There she has a view of Rock Harbor and the offshore islands "as well as an extended view of the Lake in the direction of home sweet home which brought up to fond memory many reminiscences of home & friends." On that spot, at that moment, she finds herself isolated not only in space but also in time: "I was particularly struck with the ragged appearance of the rocks, which lie in crumbled, weather beaten masses, one above another, presenting the appearance of having withstood the frost and storms of this Northern clime for ages." No doubt Ruth wondered then how well she would withstand the winter and, given the sense of passing time that opens and closes the journal, how brief her time would be in comparison to the ages the island has endured.

Nonetheless, despite Ruth's sense of unease and isolation, she often rebounds from these moments of depression. Dependent at first upon the availability of her husband and a rowing crew to take her on outings—the harbor is the easy means of getting around, far less daunting than the rugged terrain of the island with only the faintest of Indian portage trails or rough mining roads—she soon (October 4) recruits a "half-breed" woman to take her and her friend Mrs. Matthews sailing ("she managed the boat just as well as a man") and finds pride in their independence and mobility ("quite pleased with our trip, feeling very independent that we were able to go out alone"). She can be amused by the bustle the arrival of a vessel provokes ("I think Ransom should be classed among the Seaport Towns" [October 19]), despite its being the occasion for departure of one of her most frequent companions. Although the imminent isolation of winter preys on everyone's mind, she struggles to come to terms with the situation. At one point she writes, "To me, this is a gloomy idea, however, if it is to be so, I can not help it, and I will endeavor to submit without murmuring" (November 4). Later she observes, "It is a dark and rainy day, but with my needle and Books, I find no time to get lonely. I recollect an old adage that 'when the hands are busily employed the mind is content' . . . if I was not engaged with something to take up my time I should be very miserable" (November 22). She describes her usual routine as "sewing, reading, writing, eating, &c. &c" and is grateful for their "choice library, with which to employ our leisure moments" and to provide them "a source of amusement and profit" (December 26).

The circumstances of separation from her family and friends in Detroit and enforced isolation by location and climate were compounded for Ruth by her status in the island community. In Detroit, social activities took a significant role in the daily lives of women like Ruth, particularly when they lived in households of some affluence and prominence. She has very little to say in her journal about daily routines, in part because they may simply be too routine or too predictable—part of her avoidance of "the design of the author" is eschewing the faithful record keeping of diarists bent on preserving even the minutest trivia—but also in part because her social position never required her to be very active in daily routines. In Detroit, prior to her marriage, she had shared a household with two wealthy uncles, her mother, and her older sister; after her marriage she continued to live at either her uncles' house or at a commercial residence, a boarding house or hotel, where servants were employed; in Walworth, Wisconsin, where she spent the early months of 1848, she was in the household of her husband's parents, with unmarried sisters-in-law still living at home and married sisters-in-law nearby; and on Isle Royale, as the superintendent's wife, she may well have had the services of company employees to perform some of the domestic duties. Certainly Ruth gives little indication of active participation in domestic chores—when she writes of Thanksgiving that "[w]e had a very good dinner, such an one, as I should not be ashamed of, in any place, and fourteen guests to partake of it" (November 27), she does not actually suggest that she prepared the meal herself. Rather, she seems to suggest that while certain benefits of more developed settlements are denied them (for example, she frequently regrets the impossibility of sleighing), by and large they have little to complain of materially: "We have as many of the comforts of life here, as we should enjoy in almost any place. many more than one would supose that had had no experience in this new country. We have as yet a plenty of fresh meats, such as, Beef, Fish, Fowls, Rabbits, &c., &c., together with as good vegetables as one would wish to find in any places, also a sufficiency of nicknacks. in short everything for our health and comfort" (December 25). This secure position was a mixed blessing: while it may have prevented her from having to endure the drudgery more typical of a woman's life on the frontier—the daily round of physical chores, cooking, cleaning, mending, childrearing, and tending to livestock—it also created a wider gulf between the life she had left behind and the life she lived on the island. Columbus spent his days dealing with the maintenance of the mining operation, supervising the smelter, visiting the various sites, solving the problems of men and equipment which arose daily; Ruth's days were often what she made of them.

It is often difficult to conjecture confidently from Ruth Douglass's comments—for example, we simply do not know the size of her living quarters and whether her statement about the first floor indicates it was a two-story structure (as was built at the Siskowit Mine location). At the same time, although one should be cautious about assuming too much from what Ruth Douglass *does not* mention in her journal, the very fact that she says nothing about domestic chores and responsibilities in the entries on Detroit and Walworth and mentions only sewing on Isle Royale suggests that her household labor was limited. While we might make assumptions based on more general views of the roles women played in the life of established cities and in the development of frontier communities, generalizing too broadly also has risks. One writer has observed that, in this pioneering period, "all travel writers defined the married man as the instigator of continual family mobility and the married woman as the unhappy follower: men were discontented when not moving or planning a move, and women were socially isolated by the results of continual movement."[1] But such a view overlooks the evidence of the women involved in such migrations themselves. Those who have studied the diaries, journals, and letters of pioneer women have discovered that, as in the case of women settlers on the western mining and ranching frontiers, "most of these women were in the West or were doing what they were doing of their own volition. They had *chosen* to go or to do that work."[2] Certainly Ruth Douglass's own account of the conversation in which her husband discussed moving to Isle Royale couched his request as one she could refuse. As Julie Roy Jeffrey has observed generally about western emigration, "despite an ideology assigning men the responsibility for making economic decisions, women also participated in decision-making and shared men's opportunism."[3] In "the concept of domesticity" prevalent throughout the period, the ability of women to "find fulfillment at home . . . depended in some measure upon their husbands' economic success."[4] Moreover, because "the family provided meaning for women's lives and the basis for self-esteem, women might well wish to cooperate with emigration plans."[5] In the case of the Douglasses, Ruth was well aware of Columbus's "backwoods life" throughout the ten years preceding their marriage. He had spent a portion of every year since 1840 in the Upper Peninsula—indeed was in that region both before and after their wedding—and would spend some weeks on the road during the winter and summer of 1848.

The pattern of that first year of marriage, from August 1847 to August 1848, presented Ruth with an alternative when C. C. made his request. After all, "it was common practice for nineteenth-century men to leave their wives for months or even years at a time for the sake of their work; there were businessmen in city boarding houses whose families lived in the country or in small towns elsewhere, engineers on mining or railroad expeditions, politicians in distant legislatures."[6] Ruth Douglass had already experienced one of the "culturally acceptable alternatives" to migrating, and while on Isle Royale would encounter other women who had chosen them. In 1848–1849, Cornelius Shaw's family wintered over with him on Isle Royale, but the previous year Shaw had spent the entire summer alone on the island. Ruth's closest companion, Mrs. Matthews, apparently arrived on the island after Ruth did and left with her husband in late autumn, but Mark Matthews had been in charge of the company's location all year prior to C. C. Douglass's arrival.

Moreover, in both her family and that of her husband, she could trace a history of moving west almost state by state and generation by generation, one generation finding a new place to develop and settle down and the next going off in search of new opportunities opening up further west. Ruth's father had been born in Bennington, Vermont; her mother had been born in East Windsor, Connecticut; Ruth and her siblings were born in Sangerfield, New York.[7] Her husband's father had been born in New London, Connecticut, moved with his parents to Wallingford, Vermont, and settled in Springville, New York; Columbus and most of his siblings were born in New York and raised in Macomb County, Michigan, before the family moved on to settle in Wisconsin.[8] When family history is considered, and the active roles that certain Newberrys and Douglasses played in the social and commercial life of the communities in which they settled, the prospects for the life Ruth might have lived beyond the year on Isle Royale seemed to have been full of promise.

Ruth's parents belonged to farming families in Oneida County, New York. Isaac H. Edgerton and Louisa Newberry were married on January 14, 1819, and they eventually had three children. Their first child, Fanny L. Edgerton, was born December 18, 1819, and their only son, Oliver N. Edgerton, was born January 20, 1822. Their youngest child, Ruth Warner Edgerton, named for both her grandmother and her mother's surviving sister, was born September 30, 1824. The children grew up in the rural community of Sangerfield, an area notable for farming hops and cattle. Schools had been established with the formation of the township in 1795 and the Edgerton children were probably educated in those schools. The family is listed on census records for Oneida County for 1820 and 1830 as working in agriculture. Sometime before 1840 they moved to nearby Madison County, where Isaac Edgerton died of consumption in Bridgeport on March 3, 1842, at the age of fifty-three.

At Isaac's death Louisa was nearly fifty-six, and her children were adults. Fanny was twenty-two, Oliver was twenty, and Ruth was eighteen. As a widow Louisa Edgerton had several options: she could try to make a life for herself in central New York; she could move to the Sangerfield farm with her widowed father, Amasa Newberry, and her younger brother, also named Amasa; or she could turn to two older brothers living in Detroit, who seem to have been more than willing to take in both her and her children. By 1842 Oliver Newberry, a lifelong bachelor, and Henry Newberry, a widower with two children of his own, were both prominent, wealthy merchants with community standing and social connections. Louisa Edgerton took Fanny, Oliver, and Ruth to Detroit, where Oliver Edgerton was soon employed by his uncles and, within a few years, Ruth Edgerton married Columbus C. Douglass.

The Backwoods Life of C. C. Douglass

When, in August 1848, C. C. Douglass told Ruth about the offer he had received to "establish a smelting works" on Isle Royale, she recorded his observation that he had "led something of a back woods life." Indeed, his occupation over the previous decade had kept him in the least-settled regions of the state.

Columbus Christopher Douglass was born in Springville, New York, in 1812. His parents, Christopher Douglass and Phoebe Douglass, Christopher's second cousin, had ten children and moved to Macomb County, Michigan, in 1827, where they bought land near Mt. Clemens. In the 1830 Michigan Territorial Census the family was listed in Clinton Township. Mt. Clemens became a familiar family area; the Douglasses' oldest child, Aurilla, married and farmed in the county until her death. During the time the Douglasses were in Michigan it is likely that they had occasion to interact with the Newberrys in the Detroit area. Christopher Douglass's property in Mt. Clemens was in the same county as Ruth's uncle Elihu Newberry's property in Romeo, and he invested in some of the same projects in which Oliver Newberry invested. Some of C. C. Douglass's cousins, children of his father's siblings, had also established themselves in Michigan, notably Douglass Houghton, his younger brother, Jacob Houghton, Jr., the lawyer and later judge Samuel T. Douglass, and his brother, Silas H. Douglass, who followed Douglass Houghton on the faculty of the University of Michigan. By the time Ruth Edgerton arrived in Detroit, the social connections between the Douglasses and the Newberrys had been established.

Dr. Douglass Houghton had become a popular and successful figure in Detroit as a lecturer, mayor, early faculty member of the University of Michigan, and surgeon and botanist for the 1831–1832 Schoolcraft expedition to the Upper Mississippi River and Lake Superior.[9] When Michigan became a state, Houghton was appointed state geologist and initiated a survey of the state's resources. For his geological assistants, Houghton hired C. C. Douglass and Bela Hubbard, the latter of whom became an affluent Detroit businessman and wrote thoroughly and well about his experiences in Houghton's employ.[10]

In 1837, the three men and Houghton's dog, Dash, explored portions of the Lower Peninsula around Saginaw and the Thumb.[11] Much of the incentive for the survey lay in the cataloging of the resources of the new state. In succeeding years Douglass and Hubbard worked principally as surveyors for the state, mapping a number of counties in the Lower Peninsula. C. C. reported his surveys of Ingham, Eaton, and Jackson counties in the 1838 report, of Jackson, Calhoun, Kalamazoo, Eaton, Ionia, Kent, Ottawa, Van Buren, and Allegan counties in 1839, and of the "northern portion of the southern peninsula" in 1840. Reports from Douglass and Hubbard make up a considerable portion of Houghton's annual reports on the progress of the survey.[12] The balance between the scientific focus of the survey and its justification in potentially commercial applications is clear in these reports.

In addition, Douglass and Hubbard were among those who accompanied Houghton in July and August 1840 on a major expedition along the southern shore of Lake Superior from Sault Ste. Marie to La Pointe, Wisconsin. In the two published accounts of the trip—the journals of Charles W. Penny and Bela Hubbard—Douglass is a background figure. When the party spent several days at La Pointe, Wisconsin, the Indians encamped there gave animal names to the party members. Douglass was named "Me-gic" (the Otter) by one of the Indians, and it is under this title that Hubbard identified him in his sketch of Douglass in backwoods garb, the only known portrait of him.[13] The expedition was an important one for C. C. Douglass, because it established a familiarity with the Upper Peninsula copper region, the exploration of which would dominate his life for the next two decades. Until 1861 no year passed without his presence in the Upper Peninsula—on the Keweenaw Peninsula, in the Ontonagon region, or on Isle Royale.

The year following the Houghton expedition Douglass was again investigating the geology of the Ontonagon area as well as continuing his work in the Lower Peninsula.[14] The travels of Houghton's team between 1837 and 1841 produced a considerable amount of information about the potential for mining, lumbering, fishing, and farming throughout the state, especially along the coastlines of the Great Lakes, and established Columbus Douglass in his lifelong association with Upper Peninsula mining.

The geological survey was largely completed by the end of 1841, although Houghton still had not written up the final report by his death in 1845. C. C. Douglass and Jacob Houghton, Jr., were both working on the Keweenaw independently of the survey when Douglass Houghton drowned. Prior to Houghton's death, a treaty with the Ojibwas, ratified in 1843, had opened up the western end of the Upper Peninsula and Isle Royale to the possibilities of mining, and C. C. Douglass was among the geologists who began exploring for eastern mining interests. In the summer of 1844, the work of the state survey was completed and Douglass went to Sault Ste. Marie while his cousin argued in Washington for federal funding of a combined geological and lineal survey. C. C. Douglass wrote to his father and other relatives in Walworth about his prospects in the copper region, which he found promising: "There is however a Spirit of Speculation a head and the only way to make money is to ride the hobby as long as it does not Rock."[15] The letter displays the energy and ambition that fired C. C. Douglass and led him, when the prospects for the geological survey were delayed, to work for mining companies exploring the Upper Peninsula.

Indeed that very summer, Douglass began to make his presence felt in copper mining. Dr. Charles T. Jackson, who would eventually be appointed head of the United States geological survey of the region but was then working for such private firms as the Lake Superior Mining Company, reported that he was indebted to the "industry and perseverance of Mr. Douglass" for his work in locating and evaluating copper veins.[16] According to Jacob Houghton, Jr., C. C. Douglass's role was more independent than Jackson reported:

> In the summer, 1844, C. C. Douglass, formerly Assistant State Geologist of Michigan, was employed by the Lake Superior Company to explore their locations already made, and also to explore for the purpose of making further locations. During these explorations, Mr. Douglass discovered quite a number of veins, several of which have since been proved to be among the richest in the country. Mr. Douglass had the management of most of the field work for that Company.[17]

In 1845 the Lake Superior Company had "the most extensive works" in the Keweenaw region with "about 120 workmen" and "near 800 tons of ore ready for the stamping or crushing machine."[18] Jackson reported to the company's directors the "stamping and crushing mills, with the joggling tables, settling troughs, &c., were put up by Mr. C. C. Douglass . . . who has effected the work in a satisfactory manner."[19]

Columbus Douglass was apparently actively engaged in a number of projects throughout the period. Over the next decade and a half he would work for several different companies. He was involved with some of them, like the Douglass Houghton Company, for more than twenty years; others, like the Cliff Mine, employed him intermittently. In 1846 he managed sites for the Lake Superior Company and the Douglass Houghton Company. Douglass was so much a fixture of the Lake Superior region that there are offhand references to him in a number of reports and letters.[20] In addition to working with the Lake Superior and Douglass Houghton companies, he also worked with the New York and Michigan Company, and is often included among a group of men who were the first to winter over on the Keweenaw Peninsula, in 1846–1847, to develop the location. His mining claims listed his residence as Lake Superior, rather than the off-season home location other miners listed, and in addition to his other employment in 1845 he became the first postmaster of Eagle Harbor.

The commitment to the region by Columbus Douglass and his cousin Jacob Houghton encouraged other members of the Douglass family to come north. C. C.'s younger brother, Carlos Lavalette Douglass, was involved in mining in 1846 (although he had returned to Wisconsin by the time Ruth married Columbus).[21] Columbus and his brother-in-law Ransom Shelden established a store in the L'Anse area at the mouth of the Portage River and built a frame house in 1847.[22] The store was one of many enterprises that Shelden and Douglass invested in together. Over the next few decades their entrepreneurial activities would affect the growth of the region. Both men would become considerably wealthy by 1860, not only through the sale of supplies to miners and pioneers but also through the buying and selling of land and the occasional management of mines.

Such was the degree of C. C. Douglass's involvement in the Upper Peninsula that it is difficult to imagine when he found the time to meet, court, and marry Ruth Edgerton. After their wedding in August 1847, Douglass was gone on "an inspecting tour to the Ontonagon district" with John Harris Forster from early October through the end of November.[23] In a letter to Ransom Shelden at "Portage Entry, L,Ance, Lake Superior" on November 20, 1847, from Fort Wilkins at Copper Harbor, C. C. Douglass indicated that he would be going down on the *India*, and offered business advice for the coming season.[24] He made no mention that he was returning to his bride of just over three months, but his backwoods life would be a major influence on the course of their lives in the next two and a half years. After their first year of marriage, the rest of their life together would be spent in the Lake Superior mining regions.

Detroit in Mid-Century

Following Michigan's admission into statehood in 1837, the settled population of Detroit and outlying communities increased. Across the Old Northwest, especially along lakeshores and rivers, outposts swelled into cities and new cities emerged from wilderness, while further inland farmland was created from enlarged oak openings and converted prairies. Such figures as Ruth's uncles Oliver Newberry and Walter Newberry had been early developers of the cities; such figures as C. C. Douglass's father, Christopher Douglass, had been pioneers of rural communities; now a new population of American migrants and European immigrants hurried west, spurred on by the promise of fertile farmland, expanding enterprise, or mining wealth. Between the census of 1840 and the census of 1850, the recorded population of Detroit grew from 9,102 to 21,019.[25]

It was an era of transportation development as well. Regular passage across the Great Lakes was established, from Buffalo in the east to Chicago in the west, with Detroit as a major stopping point in between. Roads developed across Michigan to reach St. Joseph, where travelers could reach Chicago by booking passage to cross Lake Michigan or taking stages to skirt the top of Indiana by land. Before statehood plans had been made to follow the highways with railroads, Christopher Douglass and Oliver Newberry were both early investors. The 1850 census showed that less than one-third of Detroit's population had been born in Michigan—many listed family members born in westward-heading steps, the oldest members in England, the next generation in New York, Pennsylvania, or Ohio, only the youngest in Michigan or Wisconsin—and only a little more than half had been born in the United States: "Thousands of settlers are pouring in every year; and of these, many are Irish, Germans, or Dutch, working their way into the back country, and glad to be employed for a while at Detroit, to earn money to carry them further."[26]

The city of Detroit travelers encountered on their way west was a flourishing center of commerce but still in many ways a frontier city. In 1849 it was a city of 19,000 inhabitants, which "strung out along the river front and did not extend northward of Lafayette Avenue"; it "lay mostly between St. Antoine and Third Streets and there were only a few scattered homes as far north as Grand Circus Park. Business was confined chiefly to Jefferson Avenue, Woodbridge and Atwater Streets."[27] The muddiness of the streets impressed every traveler. Ruth Douglass mentions the difficulty people had getting about on a rainy New Year's Day, and "Helen," an otherwise anonymous letter writer passing through in 1847, remarked that Detroit "has many very pretty and some elegant situations in it but the streets are very muddy and the Citty is not lighted att all evenings excepting by the Shop windows."[28] Several plank toll roads led out Michigan, Grand River, Woodward, and Gratiot Avenues and were the main routes of stagelines connecting with towns in the interior. Homes as well as shop windows were still lighted by candles and oil lamps before the introduction of gas lighting in the next decade.

Most of the city stretched along the Detroit River, and travelers such as the English writer Harriet Martineau thought the land around Detroit "as flat as can be imagined." She claimed, "A lady of Detroit once declared, that if she were to build a house in Michigan, she would build a hill first."[29] Yet travelers were also often delighted by the social life that this otherwise rough-hewn community offered. The Swedish traveler Fredrika Bremer, visiting the city in 1850, thought Detroit looked "pleasanter and more friendly" than Buffalo, and felt that the "people of Detroit were, for the rest, pleased with their city and their way of life there, pleased with themselves, and with each other."[30] Harriet Martineau earlier had recorded "two great pleasures" on one day, "a drive along the quiet Lake St. Clair, and a charming evening party at General Mason's." She commented, "It was wholly unexpected to find ourselves in accomplished society on the far side of Lake Erie; and there was something stimulating in the contrast between the high civilisation of the evening, and the primitive scenes that we were to plunge into the next day."[31] Martineau attributed some of that social presence to the city's long history from colonial days, and her observations reinforce the sense of a flourishing social scene intimated (but hardly spelled out) in Ruth Douglass's allusions in her journal to gentlemen calling on ladies, beaux and belles, and a season for parties.

General Friend Palmer's reminiscences of early Detroit during the period in which Ruth lived there paint it as a socially active community:

> The Michigan Exchange, in the "forties," was also a famous place for the gay and dancing portion of Detroit's society, young and old, to assemble during the long winter months and "chase the hours with flying feet"; Detroit was always gay in those days, more particularly in the winter season. When the "frost king" locked the lake and river in his icy embrace, cutting off all communication from the eastern world, fun and frolic had full sway. It was here in the ballroom of this hotel, during the time the Fourth United States Infantry (Grant's regiment) was stationed here, that all Detroit's gay "400" or less, whatever there was, the creme de la creme, met in weekly cotillion parties, gotten up by subscription. That they were exclusive goes without saying.[32]

Given her uncles' standing in Detroit business, Ruth Edgerton and her siblings were likely among the company at these events, as C. C. Douglass likely was through his connection to Douglass Houghton. Elsewhere Palmer mentions that "Lake Superior magnates, the copper kings of the early days, used to make this [Michigan Exchange] their headquarters also, when in the city" and includes C. C. Douglass and his brother-in-law Ransom Shelden among those magnates he lists.[33] Although it is unclear from what period this list is drawn up, the reference reinforces the suspicion that C. C. Douglass tended to live in temporary quarters in Detroit, rather than to be regularly domiciled there, and after he and Ruth married, she may have either shared such living conditions with him or boarded with family in his absences.

The city of Detroit was expanding, with a growing number of schools, churches, libraries and literary societies, newspapers, cemeteries, hotels and taverns, and businesses. It was an important connection between the American East and West, the passenger and freight link for people and goods moving from New York and New England across the Erie Canal and Lake Erie to the mining country of Michigan's Upper Peninsula and the fertile farmlands of Wisconsin and Illinois. Particularly in the age of lake steamers, at a time when settlement tended to stay close to rivers and lake shorelines, Detroit was a vital terminus for shipping, travel, and communication. While stagelines might have been more direct and quicker for travelers who did not have to contend with the turbulence and headwinds that could make lake travel uncertain, the roads were sufficiently undeveloped that stage travel could be often treacherous and slow as well. Like the imminent development of gas lighting, two factors would change communication and travel in the immediate future—the telegraph and the railway. The telegraph was first used in Michigan between Detroit and Ypsilanti, its office "located in a rear room in the second story of a building owned by Mr. Newberry [Ruth's uncle] at the northeast corner of Jefferson Avenue and Cass Street."[34] It was completed from Detroit to Buffalo and Chicago by the end of 1848. The construction of the Michigan Central Railway had moved slowly west across the state, as far as Kalamazoo when Ruth and her husband took it in early 1848, and eventually it would extend first to Lake Michigan and then to Chicago. Though no longer the state capital in 1848, after the seat of government was moved to Lansing, Detroit was still Michigan's capital city in terms of commerce and society.

With all of the city's energy and vitality, Ruth Douglass seems to have felt fully at home here. By the time she married C. C. Douglass, she had probably been a resident of the city for several years. All of her immediate family were living with her uncle Oliver Newberry in 1850, according to census records. Oliver Newberry had established himself in Detroit after military service in the War of 1812 and an initial business enterprise in Buffalo, bringing with him several of his brothers. The Newberry brothers not only operated a store at the corner of Jefferson and Griswold but also ran a forwarding and commission business, shipping and storing merchandise passing through Detroit. To avoid paying freight rates charged by other shippers, Oliver Newberry began his own fleet of ships in 1825, and eventually established regular freight and passenger service between Detroit and Buffalo to the east, Green Bay, Milwaukee, and Chicago to the west, and Mackinac Island and Sault Ste. Marie to the north. Eventually he was referred to as "the Admiral of the Lakes" "because he was the chief vessel-builder and owner and because he established the first system of lake transportation, by steam and sail between Buffalo, Detroit and Chicago and became the first millionaire of Detroit."[35] Newberry entered into partnership with George W. Dole in Chicago, and "the firm of Newberry & Dole soon became the principal carriers of lake traffic, packers of salt meats and carriers of grain on the upper lakes."[36] In 1846 Newberry, with other lake shippers Sam Ward and E. B. Ward, led a drive to get the federal government to dredge a channel into the Chicago River. "It was the beginning of large scale river and harbors improvement and when the channel was opened Newberry's large passenger steamer, the *Illinois*, was the first vessel to enter the dredged cut and tie up in Chicago river."[37] By 1848 Oliver Newberry was one of the wealthiest and most prominent figures in the Great Lakes region.

A lifelong bachelor, Oliver maintained his closest relationship with Henry Newberry, the oldest of the Newberry siblings. Oliver lived in Henry's house on the west side of Shelby Street, between Congress and Fort, and they maintained the same household for many years before Oliver built a house of his own.[38] Their household had varying numbers of people in it. Henry was a widower raising a son and a daughter of his own, and sometime after 1842 the household included Louisa Newberry Edgerton and her three children, Fanny, Oliver, and Ruth. Possibly Ruth and Columbus made it their home base as well during their first year of marriage, a year in which one or both of them were so often away from Detroit.

Given the nature of C. C. Douglass's work and the time they spent in Wisconsin and the Upper Peninsula in the three years following their wedding, it is unlikely that the Douglasses ever had an established home in Detroit. No city directory records an address for either of them during this period, and it is likely that Ruth either continued to live with her uncles and mother or that the couple lived in a hotel, a popular residence for young couples at that time. Their visit to his parents and siblings in Walworth, Wisconsin, during the first part of 1848 may have been partly motivated by a desire to find Ruth a place to live while Columbus traveled on business and the couple made decisions about where they would establish themselves.

The Journey to Wisconsin

The first half of Ruth Douglass's 1848 diary describes her stay with her husband's family in Walworth, Wisconsin. Ruth and Columbus Douglass made the journey there by train and stagecoach; advertisements made it seem a quick and pleasant one. An 1846 ad for the Michigan Central Railroad claimed that travelers would leave Detroit at 8 A.M. and arrive at Kalamazoo at 6 P.M., passing through Ypsilanti, Ann Arbor, Dexter, Jackson, Albion, Marshall, Battle Creek, and Kalamazoo, "146 miles in 10 hours." In good weather, "B. Humphrey & Co's line of Post Coaches" would complete the route to St. Joseph, "56 miles in 12 hours," and the vessel *Champion* would take passengers across Lake Michigan to Chicago, "70 miles in 5 hours, weather permitting. Making 270 miles in about 30 hours, to and from Detroit and Chicago."[39] By the summer of 1848 the line advertised: "From Detroit to Chicago Through in 32 hours, 165 miles Cars, 40 miles Stage, 60 miles Steamboat," all for $6.50. They promised that passengers "would arrive in Chicago TWO DAYS QUICKER Than by taking the circuitous route of the Lakes."[40] Fredrika Bremer, crossing Michigan by train in September 1850, noted "small farms, with their well-built houses, surrounded by well-cultivated land"; she thought the country "monotonous," notable chiefly for occasional "small frame houses, and . . . wooden sheds, upon which a board was fastened, whereon might be read in white letters, half a yard high, the word 'Grocery'."[41]

The Douglasses found the route to be not as efficient as the advertisements claimed; it took them fifteen hours to reach Kalamazoo by train. Traveling in winter, they took the overland route from Kalamazoo to Chicago, which added forty-eight hours to the trip, and then rode for two more days over rough, frozen-mud roads from Chicago to Walworth, five days in all. Arriving around sunset, Ruth quietly observed that they were "about tired of stage riding in Winter, and quite happy to get to our journey's end" (January 14).

The roads traveled by stage coaches were rough in the best of weather. Harriet Martineau described riding by wagon across the entire width of Michigan in 1836 as a situation where "the feet are dancing an involuntary jig, all the way; while the rest of the body is in a state of entire repose."[42] Even when the roads dried they were left with deep ruts and holes and pools of water of unpredictable depth. Fredrika Bremer wrote of one stage journey that she

> was shaken, or rather hurled, unmercifully hither and thither upon the new-born roads of Wisconsin, which are no roads at all, but a succession of hills, and holes, and water-pools, in which first one wheel sank and then the other, while the opposite one stood high up in the air. Sometimes the carriage came to sudden stand-still, half overturned in a hole. . . . Sometimes we drove for a considerable distance in the water, so deep that I expected to see the equipage either swim or sink

altogether. And when we reached dry land, it was only to take the most extraordinary leaps over stocks and stones. They comforted me by telling me that the diligence was not in the habit of being upset very often![43]

It is hardly surprising under such circumstances that Ruth Douglass's most frequent term for the travel is "wearying."

Michigan, Ohio, Indiana, Illinois, and Wisconsin, the states in which the Douglasses together or C. C. Douglass alone traveled in 1848, were rapidly developing. It was "a landscape in flux," where travelers encountered "a society emerging on an unfamiliar landscape aswirl with a mobile population."[44] Caroline Kirkland, who had written memorably of her own attempt to settle in Michigan, wrote in 1845, "It is like nothing else in the wide world. . . . Language, ideas, manners, customs—all are new."[45] Ohio had become a state in 1803, when the Louisiana Purchase expanded the territory of the United States across the Mississippi River to the Pacific Northwest; Indiana and Illinois had been states since 1816 and 1818, respectively. But Michigan had only joined the union in 1837, the same year the first covered wagons reached California, and Wisconsin was admitted in 1848 (it was technically still a territory when the Douglasses visited it), when the close of the Mexican War added the rest of the western territories to the United States. Gold had already been discovered in California, and from 1849 onward the western gold rush replicated on a larger and more frantic scale the copper boom of the Upper Peninsula that C. C. Douglass had been a part of since the early 1840s.

Land speculation had made Chicago a central departure point for the migrating population; M. H. Dunlop notes, "Between 1835 and 1837 alone, 38 million acres of public land in the United States were sold, with perhaps 28 million of those acres bought as speculative investment."[46] Ruth's Detroit-based uncle, Oliver Newberry, acquired his wealth through shipping eastern goods to western communities; her Chicago-based uncle, Walter Loomis Newberry, acquired his principally through land speculation. Harriet Martineau, who arrived in Chicago in 1836, during the height of the land speculation, thought it the busiest city she had seen in America. She claimed, "The streets were crowded with land speculators, hurrying from one sale to another . . . it seemed as if some prevalent mania infected the whole people."[47] "Store-keepers" hawked farms and "all manner of land-lots" to passers-by on the street. It was a vivid and lively scene, and it led to the rapid development of the city. William Cullen Bryant, who had previously visited the city in 1841, found the changes so great in 1846, when the population had tripled over the five-year interval, that he had some difficulty in recognizing it: "It has its long rows of warehouses and shops, its bustling streets; its huge steamers, and crowds of lake-craft, lying at the wharves; its villas embowered with trees; and its suburbs, consisting of the cottages of German and Irish laborers, stretching northward along the lake, and westward into the prairies, and widening every day. The slovenly and raw appearance of a new settlement begins in many parts to disappear."[48] Bryant's image of Chicago is one of vitality and growth, but Fredrika Bremer, a few years later, thought it to be "one of the most miserable and ugly cities which I have yet seen in America . . . sitting there on the shore of the lake in wretched dishabille." She complained of the scarcity of "pretty country houses, with their gardens" and objected to the wooden houses and wooden or sandy streets. Worst of all, to her the city seemed for the most part to consist of shops; it seemed "as if, on all hands, people came here merely to trade, to make money, and not to live."[49]

Ruth and Columbus Douglass passed through Chicago and took an inland route through northern Illinois to Walworth County, but on their return trip they hoped first to travel by steamer, now that it was late enough in the year for the lakes to be open. At mid-century both stagecoaches and ships traveled up the western coast of Lake Michigan from Chicago to Sheboygan and Green Bay. When the stormy weather discouraged them from taking passage on the steamer *Manhattan*, the Douglasses returned to Chicago down the coast by stage, then found safer lake passage on Oliver Newberry's ship, the *Michigan*, which returned them up the coast of Wisconsin before crossing the lake to the Straits of Mackinaw and the sail down Lake Huron to Detroit.

"It is surprising how many persons travel, as way-passengers, from place to place on the shores of these lakes," William Cullen Bryant observed, claiming that "they comprise, at least, half the number on board a steamboat plying between Buffalo and Chicago." Along the coast, cities were springing up with hopes of rivaling Chicago as ports of call—Little Fort (later renamed Waukegan) in Illinois, South Port (now Kenosha) in Wisconsin, and, most impressively, Milwaukee, which Bryant felt was "rapidly becoming one of the great cities of the West," commending its "several large and lofty warehouses" and "an hotel of the largest class."[50] Fredrika Bremer thought Milwaukee "beautiful" and admired its location ("a charming situation on elevated ground"), its architecture ("ornamental without pomp"), and its aspirations ("increases with all its might"), concluding that "Milwaukee, not Chicago, deserves to be called 'Queen of the Lake'."[51]

Most of Ruth Douglass's time in Wisconsin was spent on Big Foot Prairie, a broad, flat expanse of cultivated land that extended across portions of southern Wisconsin and northern Illinois. The prairie had been "broken" by settlers ten years earlier, in good measure by her father-in-law, who had brought the only team of oxen to the county and was able to plow furrows two and a half miles long, right up to the state line. When he had established a farm site, Christopher Douglass sent for his wife and children in Illinois. Their property, a few miles from the state line, came to be known as Douglass Corners and would eventually evolve into the village of Walworth, platted by Ruth's brother-in-law Carlos Lavalette Douglass. Lavalette would go on to become a force in the development of the county, partly through the establishment of Big Foot Mills in nearby Fontana, at the head of Lake Geneva. Two other brothers, Gilbert Lafayette Douglass and Oscar Houghton Douglass, would also establish farms in the county. By the time Ruth arrived in the area, Christopher Douglass had built the Red Lion Tavern, a regular stop on the stagecoach route. He had also moved a building to his land to serve as a school. Eventually his property would serve as the basis for the Walworth town square. The local post office was located further northwest up the road between Chicago and Madison, at Bell's Corners, and on good days it was a pleasant two-mile walk across cultivated prairie.[52]

When Ruth Douglass visited Walworth, the Douglass family had already been settled on the land for a decade. "The Prairie bears every resemblance to an old settled country," Ruth noted on February 1. "On every side you turn your eye you behold large cultivated fields neatly fenced, also good buildings as one sees in passing through almost any farming district, even in the state of New York." It was perhaps that feeling of this being an old settled country that made Christopher Douglass long to move further west. When he had arrived on the prairie, a decade before, it had been open and empty. About that time, Harriet Martineau, after a tour of the prairie from Chicago to Joliet, remarked of prairie life: "I never saw insulation, (not desolation,) to compare with the situation of a settler on a wide prairie. A single house in the middle of Salisbury Plain would be desolate. A single house on a prairie has clumps of trees near it, rich fields about it; and flowers, strawberries, and running water at hand. But when I saw a settler's child tripping out of home-bounds, I had a feeling that it would never get back again. It looked like putting out into Lake Michigan in a canoe."[53] By the time Ruth visited Wisconsin, the area was sufficiently developed to have regular stage service through Walworth between Southport on the coast and Beloit in the interior. Fredrika Bremer, traveling from Milwaukee to Madison in 1850, noted the development of the interior: "Many incomparably lovely lakes, with romantic shores, are scattered through this district, and human habitations are springing up along them daily."[54] In the scant two years between Ruth's visit to Wisconsin and Bremer's, the telegraph had already been widely established. Bremer commented, "It is remarkable that in all directions throughout this young country, along these rough roads, which are no roads at all, run these electric wires from tree to tree, from post to post, along the prairie-land, and bring towns and villages into communication."[55] The pace of change was already accelerating.

Ruth Douglass's few months wintering in Walworth, Wisconsin, brought her in touch with the expanding settlements of the Midwest. She had grown up in a more settled farm region in central New York and had lived in an established and growing city during her years in Detroit. Now she experienced the more sparsely populated and far-flung society that spread itself thin across the prairies, where young people went off to a party a dozen miles away and weekly mail delivery slowed down the social and business whirl. The social circle here was circumscribed by family and neighbors, unlike the extended society of friends and acquaintances she had experienced in Detroit. It must have seemed a bucolic, pastoral retreat from the bustle in the city, and the trip home with its stops in Chicago and Milwaukee and the companionship of her uncle Oliver on a crowded steamship must have seemed like going through stages of re-entry into the lifestyle of the city, a process of re-acclimation.

In reality, however, the time in Wisconsin was only a "test run" for the kind of "insulation" Harriet Martineau described. Martineau meant that living on prairie farms was like being stranded on an island in a sea—or Great Lake—of grass. By the end of August Ruth would be "insulated"— "islanded"—in a far more literal and limiting way.

The Journey to the Copper Country

Ruth Douglass wrote nothing in her journal between June 17 and August 1. She began writing again when her husband broached the subject of moving to the Upper Peninsula, where she would spend the rest of the year and, indeed, the remainder of her life.

The first portion of the journey north was a well-traveled route by 1848. Steamboats shuttled regularly between Chicago and Detroit, replenishing the fuel for their boilers on offshore wooding stops like the Manitou Islands in Lake Michigan and the Thunder Bay Islands in Lake Huron. The mainland coastline of Michigan was still undeveloped—one traveler to the mining district complained of the Manitou Islands and the mainland shore that they "present a baran [*sic*] and gloomy appearance . . . covered with dwarf pine or Stunted Cedar or hemlock" and although other "passengers

tried to see beauty in the Manatue [*sic*] Islands and the evergreen that covered everything," he confessed that "it was but little beauty I could get out
of it."[56] But the islands were busy places and frequently visited.

Mackinac Island served as the principal port of call between Port
Huron, Michigan, at the conjunction of Lake Huron and the St. Clair River,
and Sheboygan, Wisconsin, on the western shore of Lake Michigan. It was
also already a tourist destination in its own right, a flourishing way station
in the trade between the Upper Peninsula and the cities of the Great Lakes,
and a jumping-off place for excursions to Sault Ste. Marie and Lake
Superior. Mackinac Island had been, as William Cullen Bryant described
it, "known to history for the past two centuries."[57] Although Bryant recommended it as "a place that was finished, where [one] might live in peace,"
he thought its "cool summer climate" could make it "a fashionable watering-place, in which case it must yield to the common fate of American villages and improve, as the phrase is."[58] Charles Lanman, whose path crossed
Bryant's that summer, thought that, "like too many of the beautiful places
on our western frontier, Mackinaw is now in a transition state. . . . its aboriginal glory is rapidly departing, and it will soon be the fashionable resort
of summer travellers."[59]

Both writers were struck by the bustle of both Mackinac Island and
Sault Ste. Marie. Bryant stayed one night at the Mission House, "a plain,
comfortable old house," and complained that the "place was crowded with
people on their way to the mining region of Lake Superior, or returning
from it, and we were obliged to content ourselves with narrow accommodations for the night."[60] On one journey on the steamer General Scott
between Sault Ste. Marie and Mackinac Island, Bryant observed "about
forty passengers on board, men in search of copper-mines, and men in
search of health, and travellers from curiosity, Virginians, New Yorkers,
wanderers from Illinois, Indiana, Massachusetts, and I believe several other
states." At the Mansion House, where they also stayed, accommodations
were crowded: "We were packed for the night almost as closely as the
Potawottamies, whose lodges were on the beach before us. Parlors and garrets were turned into sleeping-rooms; beds were made on the floors and in
the passages, and double-bedded rooms were made to receive four beds."[61]

The traffic at Mackinac Island thinned considerably as it moved
north. One traveler recorded taking the steamer *Detroit* to Sault Ste. Marie
from Mackinac Island in July 1848: "Passed a miserable night, slept with
my clothes on to keep the Bedbugs off." The following morning, rising
before 5 o'clock, he saw "the waiters take the blankets off the beds, and put
them on the breakfast table to make the Sheets which served for tablecloths
feel at home. this somewhat took off the edge of my appetite."[62]

As a destination for travelers, Sault Ste. Marie was a little more difficult of access, and it generally marked the northernmost terminus for
tourists, who found travel beyond the head of the St. Mary's River, across
Lake Superior, more challenging and less accommodating, not to mention
less available. By 1848 several vessels had been either hauled across the
portage at Sault Ste. Marie or built on the shores of Lake Superior, but the
proposed canal had not yet begun to be built and would not be completed
until 1855. One of the pleasant adventures to be had in the area was shooting the rapids under the hand of a local Indian or voyageur, but the falls and
rapids that gave the Sault its name were not navigable by heavier vessels
and eventually a strap railway line ran through the main street of the town
for transporting goods from one vessel to another. Part of the prohibitive
cost of getting copper and iron ore to market was the slow, expensive
process of crossing the Sault Ste. Marie portage. The completion of the
canal would greatly increase the speed of shipping and the flow of vessels
among the lakes and reduce the exclusivity of the Lake Superior fleet.

The approach to Sault Ste. Marie through the islands of the upper
Lake Huron and the lower St. Mary's River was, in Bryant's words, "a
winding voyage of sixty miles, between wild banks of forest, in some
places smoking with fires, in some looking as if never violated either by
fire or steel." The crowd at the Sault Ste. Marie landing consisted of "men
of all ages and complexions, in hats and caps of every form and fashion,
with beards of every length and color"; they included "copper-mine speculators, just flitting from Copper Harbor and Eagle River, mixed with a few
Indian and half-breed inhabitants of the place" and "a face or two quite
familiar in Wall-street."[63] Bryant, who had visited the place before, was
struck by the changes it had undergone: "[S]ince the world has begun to
talk of the copper mines of Lake Superior, settlers flock into the place; car-
penters are busy knocking up houses with all haste on the government
lands, and large warehouses have been built upon piles driven into the shal-
lows of the St. Mary. Five years hence, the primitive character of the place
will be altogether lost, and it will have become a bustling Yankee town,
resembling the other settlements of the West."[64] Lanman, too, found it "a
village of considerable business," particularly in the summer when it
became "one of the busiest little places in the country" and recommended
that "the contemplated ship canal through this place (which would allow a
boat from Buffalo to discharge her freight or passengers at Fond du Lac)
ought not to be delayed a single year."[65]

At Mackinac Island and at Sault Ste. Marie, a society existed that,
although reduced from the proportions she would have experienced at

Detroit, Ruth Douglass still would have recognized. People came to call on visitors and returned calls from them. Although limited and certainly emphasizing the business concerns and frontier interactions of the region, the social world of both communities emulated that of the larger cities. But beyond Sault Ste. Marie, the towns and villages being established owed their existence almost entirely to the mining trade, especially those on the Keweenaw Peninsula and along the southern shore of Michigan as far as La Pointe in Wisconsin. Copper Harbor, Eagle River, Eagle Harbor, and Ontonagon all began as landing and shipping areas for mining operations. The society in all those places centered around the principal business, and it would be a long while before these settlements developed into communities with identities separate from—or at least not wholly dependent upon—the mining operations nearby. Part of the remoteness of these places could be attributed to their distance from the settled communities of the Lower Peninsula, the inland farming communities, and the commercial cities along the shoreline. Ruth Douglass had good reason to suppose that her stay on Isle Royale would be not only physically uncomfortable but also socially isolated, particularly for the mining superintendent's wife in a location where few men brought women and few intended to stay beyond the onset of winter.

To William Cullen Bryant, Sault Ste. Marie was the "remotest settlement of the northwest,"[66] but he had not crossed Lake Superior to the Keweenaw Peninsula and the copper communities of Copper Harbor, Eagle River, and Ontonagon. The Keweenaw was remote enough that wintering over by men like C. C. Douglass and other mining explorers and developers in 1846 would be remembered by others for years. Remoter still was the island of Isle Royale.

Mining on Isle Royale

The interest in Isle Royale as a potential source of copper dates back before the Revolutionary War. The rumor of copper was a factor in determining that the island, settled in the curve of the north shore of Lake Superior, a scant fifteen miles from Canadian soil, would be included as American territory in the treaty with the British and assigned to the Michigan territory, fifty miles away. Following statehood, the Michigan Geological Survey was designed to identify and record the purposes to which the land included in the state of Michigan could be put. When Douglass Houghton's 1840 expedition investigated the prospects around the Keweenaw Peninsula and the southern shore of Lake Superior, Houghton himself ventured out to Isle Royale, where the American Fur Company had established fishing outposts, and circled the island to confirm its possibilities.

In the intervening years, as the state geological survey wound down, increasing interest in the mining potential of the region was held in abeyance until the 1843 treaty with the Chippewas surrendered their land for occupation and sale by the United States government. By 1844 prospectors were in the territory. Among them was C. C. Douglass, no longer an assistant to his cousin, but a freelance consultant to mining companies. We do not know when C. C. Douglass first explored Isle Royale, but we do know that mining sites were being explored in 1843, 1844, and 1845. Mining began in earnest in 1846, on a seasonal basis, with men coming onto the island in May and leaving it in October or November. By 1847, when Charles T. Jackson arrived to lead a geological survey for the federal government, mining sites ringed the island.

The company that hired C. C. Douglass as superintendent in the summer of 1848, the Isle Royale and Ohio Mining Company (also referred to as the Ohio and Isle Royale Mining Company), was one of the first to make claims on Isle Royale. As early as 1843, the company sent a geologist named John Locke to survey the island. Preliminary explorations were conducted in 1844 and 1845. The period of greatest activity began in 1846, when the company sent Professor J. Lang Cassels to investigate the geology and the mineralogy of "the mineral lands of Isle Royale." His report was highly encouraging, to say the least, and perhaps indicated a desire to tell the directors what they hoped to hear. For example, describing "mountain ranges of considerable magnitude, running generally longitudinal with the Island," he identified "several beautiful small lakes, affording abundant water power on their outlets, for all mining and smelting purposes." Explaining that the topography of the island made the north shore "mostly composed of perpendicular bluffs and cliffs," while the south shore had "a gradual rocky declination to the water's edge," he argued that "the geological arrangement of Isle Royale" was "of immense advantage in the process of mining," because the expense of pumping out shaft water "will be avoided, as the water can be drained by *adits,* at a trifling cost."[67]

Moreover, contradicting reports "by those who have cursorily viewed its rock-bound shore" and described the island "as a barren waste, incapable of supporting vegetable life," Cassels maintained that "the soil in many places [is] susceptible of cultivation, and capable of producing all kinds of kitchen vegetables and the smaller grains. I ate potatoes of a superior quality in September, grown from a few *parings* accidentally scattered in the soil in July, by the Cook." Cassels also found "patches of alluvial deposits" that were "well adapted for hay" and would produce "sufficient quantities for the use of all the domestic animals required." He added that "it may be confidentally stated, that there is abundance of food on your several locations, both for the summer's pasturage, and winter's provision, of all the cattle the Company will need for milk or labor." He claimed there was a good supply of timber and that charcoal could be obtained "in quantities sufficient to supply a well regulated smelting furnace for an indefinite period."[68] The company could hardly have asked for a more favorable report on their prospects.

Cassels's report was dated October 6, 1846, and during that previous season there had been considerable activity on the island. The following year, Leander Ransom, the agent for the company in 1846 and 1847, came up from Ohio with a party of twenty-five workmen, "tools, implements, and provisions," and, "after a tedious, boisterous and expensive voyage," arrived on Isle Royale on May 20, 1847. "From that time until the last of September," he reported, "we were constantly employed in exploring and surveying the locations—constructing roads—building shanties and procuring specimens by making examinations of the prominent veins, preparatory to more definite and extended operations." They had "established a 'general depot'" on Rock Harbor and "cut out and opened roads" north across the island, west to McCargoe's Cove, and, most ambitiously, west to Siskiwit Bay and then due north from there across the island. "Twelve shanties have been erected at such points on the different locations, as were considered convenient and suitable for present and future operations," and nine locations had been worked on. The general depot was the clearing where the town of Ransom would be constructed. Ransom left a crew on the island and returned to Cleveland in September. Final word from Isle Royale, in a letter dated November 4, informed him that "some 5 or 6 shafts had been commenced and worked, two of which were sunk from 20 to 30 feet," and that supplies for the winter had arrived.[69]

At the same time that the Isle Royale and Ohio locations were being established, the Siskowit Mine was also operating on the shore of Rock Harbor. Charles Whittlesey, the Siskowit superintendent, reported to his directors on September 27, 1847, "The Ohio and Isle Royal Co. under the management of Messrs. Ransom and Blake, have constructed or are constructing, a first rate furnace about 2 miles from our location, and I have already arranged with them to smelt our ores. This I consider a most valuable fact in relation to the prospects of this company." Whittlesey and his crew wintered over and by February 1848 could report having built "a very good house, of two stories" and intending to clear "a piece of ground for gardening."[70] On May 25, 1848, reporting that "work has progressed favorably" over the past winter, he noted that the Isle Royale and Ohio site at

Ransom had "a furnace in course of erection, only two miles distant, the most expensive portion of which is already completed" and expected to "be in operation in the course of the summer." He added the encouraging observation that the "expense of getting the mineral to the smelting works will be trifling, the mine being only 80 yards from our wharf; a flat boat can take it directly to the furnace."[71]

The smelter at Ransom then would have served not only the immediate needs of the Isle Royale and Ohio Company but also those of other companies on the island. The cost of shipping ore down to smelters in Michigan and Ohio, particularly with the additional cost of transferring the ore to portage the Sault, was a problematic element of mining the Upper Peninsula. When copper prices fell and costs increased, it was a factor in closing down locations that initially seemed promising but could not return investors' expenses sufficiently to continue.

Some sense of the difficulty and expense of copper mining in the Upper Peninsula was provided by Horace Greeley for readers of the *New York Daily Tribune*. The editor had been on the propeller from Sault Ste. Marie with the Douglasses and had disembarked on the Keweenaw to check into mining ventures there. His report on copper mining was datelined "Eagle Harbor, Mich., Sept. 1, 1848," and his explanation of the long process of creating a successful mine applies to not only the Cliff Mine, from which he was writing, but also those mines on Isle Royale that "have hardly justified, as yet, the sanguine expectations at first formed by their explorers, but they seem to be improving." Greeley explained that "probably next season" after explorations determined a site,

> workmen, a team, provisions, powder, mining tools, &c., &c., are landed at the most convenient point on the Lake, a trail cut back to the vicinity of the discovered vein or veins, and a part of the force build some sort of dwellings, while others are setting up the indispensable blacksmith's forge, hauling up the stores, (the most necessary first,) &c. As soon as possible, the vein is probed farther, by pickaxe, drilling, and blasting; but if the force consists of only three or four men, they are not likely to penetrate the earth beyond twenty feet the first season.—Soon water begins to pour in, especially after storms, and still more abundantly in the thawing season, and arrangements must be made for its removal. . . . What with making road, building, getting up provisions, iron, tools, &c., cutting wood, timber, and the like, of the first five thousand days' work done on a location, only from one to two thousand, except under peculiar circumstances, can be devoted to mining; but at length, if the work is prosecuted, the shaft has obtained a depth of forty to sixty feet, at which is commenced a *drift*—a horizontal gallery or excavation in the rock, following the

course of the vein (usually both ways from the shaft) and from six to seven feet high, and four to six feet wide. The rock is not merely to be blasted out but raised to the surface by such rude machinery as may be at command, with probably a hundred lifts of water to one of rock.[72]

Greeley considered "$50,000 a moderate estimate for the cost of opening a mine in this region, counting from the location to the moment at which the mine will pay its way, and including the cost of land." He included in that estimate the excavation of several shafts, construction of considerable machinery to raise tons of rock, stamping mills to separate copper from rock in veinstone, and the effort involved to move copper masses "to the Lake, thence taking the propeller to the Sault, and so on to Pittsburgh or Baltimore." Given the difficulties and expense of such an enterprise, the prospect of a working smelter on Isle Royale could only encourage a more certain return on the investments in the island companies.[73]

The longest established company on the island was the Isle Royale and Ohio. Charles T. Jackson reported in 1847 that the company

now employs about fifty men, and has made great improvements at Rock Harbor—erected good buildings, cleared a large area of land, made a good garden, through which a brook flows, and is crossed in the middle by a good bridge. The soil is fertile, producing most of the ordinary culinary vegetables in abundance. It is probable, if mining operations should prove advantageous on Isle Royale, that a village will spring up in this place; and, since the improvements alluded to were first made by Mr. Leander Ransom, of Cleveland, the place is properly named, in his honor, "Ransom."[74]

Jackson noted in his journal for August 13, 1847, that "Mr. Ransom's family had arrived and his house was nearly complete."[75] This was the house that the Douglasses lived in on the island.

Ransom served as the principal port of call on the island, and the arrival of a vessel—or at least the expectation of the arrival of a vessel—could fill the small community. Miners from other sites around the island showed up to check mail and receive provisions, to greet new workers, company officials on inspection tours, family members, friends, and visitors, or simply to watch the bustle. As the season grew late, seasonal workers departed, reducing the community. In her journal entry for October 19, Ruth Douglass observed, "People from all the different locations assemble here whenever a boat comes in, and some of them make it a port of holiday. I think Ransom should be classed among the Seaport towns."

The summer and fall of 1848 was the most active on the island. A number of operations begun in 1847 were expanding and flourishing. As Lawrence Rakestraw has succinctly described the situation,

> Many of the mining locations consisted of only one or two log cabins. The more substantial settlements—those at Ransom, Siskowit Mine, Snug Harbor, and Todd Harbor—followed a standard pattern. The agent resided in a house of squared logs, while miners lived in crude log cabins. At the Siskowit Mine, in addition, a dozen single workers lived in a combination storehouse and barracks. The grass and vegetation around the settlements was burned to keep accidental fires from destroying the place. Vegetable gardens of potatoes, peas, lettuce, and radishes were grown at Snug Harbor, Ransom, and Siskowit Mine, while the Siskowit operation had extensive hay pastures for their horses. Fish, potatoes, and tea were staples of the miners' diet, supplemented with beef brought in from the mainland.[76]

The Siskowit operation began in earnest in the summer of 1847, under the direction of Charles Whittlesey. Their location was a few miles up Rock Harbor from Ransom. Beyond the Siskowit Mine was the Smithwick Mine, managed by Cornelius G. Shaw and located at Snug Harbor. The Scoville Mine was further out on Scovill Point. The Isle Royale and Ohio Mining Company had two locations on the south shore of the island between Rock Harbor and Chippewa Harbor, the Datholite and Epidote mines. There were also operations in Siskowit Bay, Washington Harbor, Duncan's Bay, Blake Point, and, on the north shore, the Pittsburg and Isle Royale Mining Company at Todd Harbor, managed by H. H. McCulloch. A number of these mines continued work during the winter of 1847–1848 and several of them continued into 1849. The winter of 1848–1849 seems to have been the turning point for the first Isle Royale mining boom. During and after the mining season of 1849 most of the sites on the island were either downsized to smaller, more focused operations or abandoned altogether.

In 1849, when the Siskowit Mining Association reorganized as the Siskowit Mining Company, they sent a new superintendent, mine captain, and "corps of miners" to the island, and "owing to the backwardness of the season" they arrived on June 1. Work had been suspended and the men had to spend part of the season restoring conditions for working and living and "freeing the old shaft and drift from water before anything at mining could be done."[77] In 1850 the German mining engineer C. L. Koch visited the site and noted that "ten miners were employed, and thirty odd people in surface work."[78]

In August of 1851 Philadelphia businessman Anton Myers "[w]ent down a shaft in a kibbel or Bucket to view very rich indications of stamp work & some masses" at the Siskowit Mine, reporting that he found the mine "in full activity, with 52 men profitably engaged—some in stamping with the new mill recently erected, some at blasting, some at the underground and some at the surface work."[79] The mine finally closed in 1855, but not until one of the veins was "sunk past six levels to a depth of about 500 feet" and the mine produced 150 tons of copper.[80]

At Todd Harbor in 1849 the Pittsburg and Isle Royale Company sank two shafts, one to the depth of 63 feet, one to 67 feet, and connected them on the second level with an adit 113 feet long.[81] The veins were profitable enough that the company could continue working them until 1853.[82] The Pittsburg and Isle Royale and the Siskowit were the only two operations to achieve sustained development. The other mines proved unprofitable.

The Smithwick Mine, Cornelius Shaw's location at Snug Harbor, is not mentioned as operational in Foster and Whitney's report to Congress. They note, speaking of changes in veins, that "Mr. Shaw sank a shaft on a vein, above Scovill's Point, to the depth of ninety-six feet" but, after a promising start, "the vein contracted to a foot in width, and was nearly barren and worthless."[83] We know that Shaw and his family, along with H. H. McCullough of the Pittsburg and Isle Royale, arrived in Sault Ste. Marie on the Algonquin on October 13, 1849, and his departure seems to have ended the mine's operation.

The Isle Royale and Ohio smelting furnace completed under the direction of C. C. Douglass never achieved its promise; ore sent from the Siskowit Mine, "either from some defect in the furnace, or want of skill in the smelter," ended up being "badly smelted."[84] Thus the Isle Royale and Ohio Company had no luck in cutting shipping costs for their own ore. When Foster and Whitney visited the Isle Royale and Ohio Company locations in the fall of 1849, they found the "operations of the company are at present confined to testing a vein on the southeast quarter of section 34, township 66, range 34, about two miles south of Rock Harbor, by the lake shore," which they thought looked favorable and seemed "sufficiently rich to pay for mining." However, four shafts "sunk by this company, under the direction of Mr. Douglass," one to 35 feet, two to 40 feet, and one to 90 feet, "at the time of our visit, were filled with water, and we were unable to gather exact information as to the character and productiveness of the several veins."[85] When Anton Myers visited the island in 1851, he and his party were rowed from the Siskowit site "down the bay for 3 miles to a mine that is abandoned from mismanagement; much money has been expended on it in buildings & machinery to no avail."[86] A family there "treated us with a nice lunch & some milk"; they were the only residents of Ransom.

"Banished to a Desolate Island"

The remoteness and isolation of Isle Royale and the severity of Lake Superior winters daunted many of the travelers to the region. Lanman, who had traveled extensively throughout the region, wrote of the climate that the winters "are very long, averaging about seven months, while spring, summer and autumn are compelled to fulfill their duties in the remaining five" and that "the snow frequently covers the whole country to the depth of three, four and five feet." Moreover, because of the snow, the "few white people who spend their winters in this remote region are almost as isolated as the inhabitants of Greenland," getting news "from the civilized world" only once a month, brought to them by mail carriers "who travel through the pathless wilderness in a rude sledge drawn by dogs." "Excepting an occasional picketed fort or trading house," Lanman observed, the Lake Superior region "is yet a perfect wilderness."[87]

Even in warmer seasons, the region was not easy traveling. Around the lakeshore the terrain was irregular and rocky. Reporting on Isle Royale in 1850, Foster and Whitney concluded that the "physical obstructions to a successful exploration of the interior island are greater than we have encountered in any other portion of the mineral district."

> The shores are lined with dense but dwarfed forests of cedar and spruce, with their branches interlocking and wreathed with long and drooping festoons of moss. While the tops of the trees flourish luxuriantly, the lower branches die off and stand out as so many spikes, to oppose the progress of the explorer. So dense is the interwoven mass of foliage that the noonday sunlight hardly penetrates it. The air is stifled; and at every step the explorer starts up swarms of musquitoes, which, the very instant he pauses, assail him. Bad as this region is by nature, man has rendered it still worse. Fires have swept over large tracts, consuming the leaves and twigs and destroying the growth, while the heavy winds have prostrated the half-charred trunks, and piled them up so as to form almost impenetrable barriers.[88]

Except for the roads opened by the mining companies and some Indian trails, the interior of the island seemed sufficiently uninviting to encourage most of the people there to stay close to the shoreline and to travel as often as possible by boat, a possibility reduced by the uncertainties of lake travel. Even C. C. Douglass, who had already wintered over once on the Keweenaw Peninsula and who was as familiar and well traveled in the region as anyone, referred to the job on Isle Royale as being "banished to a desolate island."

Both of the Douglasses had personal evidence of the perils of the region in the drowning of Columbus's cousin and the deaths of Ruth's uncles, and they had witnessed the dangers of lake travel during the tremendous storm Ruth recorded in April 1848. On Lake Superior the wreck of the *Astor*, which was at the time the only vessel on the lake other than the *Algonquin*, had devastated frontier communities dependent on the delivery of winter supplies. The year before Ruth arrived, the schooner *Merchant* was sunk off Grand Island with everyone on board, and while they were on Isle Royale the *Goliath* (or *Goliah*) exploded in Lake Huron.

If reaching one's destination seemed often in doubt, fall departure from the island was also uncertain—the weather made sailing schedules unpredictable. Storms could send vessels wildly off course or force them to pick a new destination mid-voyage, or simply keep them from either leaving or entering a harbor. On his 1840 expedition, Douglass Houghton spent several days waiting to get off the island; in 1847 Charles Jackson and his party began "hourly expecting the steamboat to Keweenaw Point" on August 12 and, after exhausting their own provisions and becoming "entirely dependent upon the hospitality of Messrs. Ransom and Blake" of the Ohio and Isle Royale Company, left the island on September 14.[89] Later that same season Cornelius Shaw "finished all preparations to leave the island" on October 7, began to "feel uneasy about the S[team] Boat not coming" on October 9, and observed by October 13 that it was "a dreary prospect to be on Isle Royale and no way to get off." Even when the schooner *Napoleon* finally arrived on October 16, it was windbound two days on the island and made the run to Copper Harbor in a gale, leaving every passenger seasick.[90]

For those less experienced in Lake Superior travel, the uncertainty must have been considerably more unnerving. Ruth reports several times in her journal the distress expressed by C. M. Giddings, a visiting director of the Isle Royale and Ohio, over the delay in leaving the island and his fear of being stranded there for the winter (as his company intended the Douglasses and its other employees to be). The anxieties expressed by Anton Myers in his 1851 journal of a trip to the copper region may be typical. Myers and his party arrived at Rock Harbor on a schooner that had been "struck with a tremendous squall which tattered her trisail to rags— the other sails were instantly loosened & all night we only drifted on bars poles, heavy thunder & lightning & rain astounding our nerves through the night"; on reaching safe harbor he marveled, "how people can be induced to bury themselves so apart from the world!" After his tour of the Siskowit Mine, he was immediately "ready & anxious for the Propellor" and he lamented, "Oh! how dejecting it is to be so separated from the world, without the power of escape unless some friendly boat should purposely come to our relief! and of this fond hope we are almost desponding since we are neglected so treacherously by those we relied upon." He noted that, because the Napoleon was "the only Propeller on the Lake," "if she comes not to our assistance in this extremity we are indeed to be pitied!" Stranded on the shoreline, he observed, "It is a melancholy sight to scan such an immense expanse of water without distinguishing a solitary being or a single sail upon it. We are indeed exiles without the means of flight!"[91] A week later, he was finally off the island and catching the vessel from Sault Ste. Marie for Detroit, immensely relieved. Ruth Douglass's mild confessions of trepidation about wintering over on the island, which crop up from time to time in her journal, seem like models of restraint and self-control compared to Myers's near-frenzy over two weeks on the island.[92]

The isolation, because it was expected, was one that had to be accepted, and it was. Ruth evaluated their situation philosophically near the end of the year, acknowledging on Christmas Day that, although they were "on a remote and lonely island . . . I forebear to repine. we are happy here, even in this solitude." In her final entry she commented that the four months they had been on the island, "which one might have supposed would have seemed long," had on the contrary "glided away almost imperceptibly." It was an outlook that no doubt served her well in the remaining, unrecorded six months of her winter on Isle Royale.

Notes

1. M. H. Dunlop, *Sixty Miles from Contentment: Traveling the Nineteenth-Century American Interior* (New York: Basic Books, 1995), 170.
2. Ruth B. Moynihan, Susan Armitage, and Christiane Fischer Dichamp, eds., *So Much to Be Done: Women Settlers on the Mining and Ranching Frontier* (Lincoln: University of Nebraska Press, 1990), xvii.
3. Julie Roy Jeffrey, *Frontier Women: The Trans-Mississippi West, 1840–1880* (New York: Hill and Wang, 1979), 31.
4. Ibid., 32.
5. Ibid., 33.
6. Moynihan, Armitage, and Dichamp, *So Much to Be Done*, xviii.
7. Ruth's maternal grandparents, Amasa Newberry (1752–1853) and Ruth Warner (1758–1815), were both born near Windsor, Connecticut. Amasa received the rank of captain during service in several units of the Continental army during the Revolutionary War, and married Ruth Warner in 1784. All of their ten children, only one of whom would not survive to adulthood, were born in Connecticut. After many years of farming a portion of the family homestead, Amasa Newberry in 1805 sold his Connecticut property and relocated the family to Sangerfield, Oneida County, New York.

   Eventually only the second youngest son, Amasa Stoughton Newberry, stayed on the Sangerfield farm. Two sons, John Warner Newberry (1799–1826) and Franklin Newberry (1795–1831), died exploring northern

Michigan. The other four sons prospered. Henry and Oliver established themselves first in Buffalo, then in Detroit, and their shipping firm became a major presence on the Great Lakes. Elihu established a tannery in Sangerfield before relocating to Romeo, Michigan, and his descendents were active in Michigan commerce and politics for several generations. Walter worked for Henry and Oliver originally but eventually established himself in Chicago, where he became wealthy and influential. Of the daughters, Ruth and Louisa both married local men, and Louisa moved out of central New York only after her husband's death. See Joseph Gardner Bartlett, *Newberry Genealogy: The Ancestors and Descendents of Thomas Newberry of Dorchester, Mass, 1634–1914* (Boston: J. G. Bartlett, 1914); Helen Bourne Joy Lee, *The Newberry Genealogy* (Chester, Conn.: Pequot Press, 1975); and the Newberry genealogy in the appendices.

   Ruth's paternal family lineage is harder to trace. Isaac Edgerton's father, Stephen Edgerton, may be the individual listed as the son of John Edgerton, Jr., and Elizabeth Prentice of Norwich in *Vital Records of Norwich, Connecticut, 1659–1848* (Hartford, Conn.: Society of Colonial Wars in the State of Connecticut, 1913), 305. He was born on May 15, 1760. Of his wife Temperance I can locate no family records. Cemetery records for Bridgeport, New York, indicate that Stephen Edgerton died on November 1, 1816; Temperance Edgerton died on June 5, 1842, at the age of eighty-five years, three months, and eighteen days, and so must have been born on March 18, 1757.

8. Like Amasa Newberry, Columbus's paternal grandfather, Daniel Douglass (1752–1821), attained the rank of captain during the Revolutionary War and wore the title to his death. On April 23, 1778, he married Lydia Douglass (1752–1811), his third cousin, like him born in New London; they had eight children while living in Connecticut and moved to Wallingford, Vermont, in 1797. By the second decade of the new century several children of Captain Daniel and Lydia Douglass had established themselves in western New York State. The eldest of two daughters, Lydia Douglass (1780–1871) married the Honorable Jacob Houghton, a lawyer from Troy, New York, in January 1806. After 1811 they lived in Fredonia, near Lake Erie. Two of their sons became prominent in Michigan, Douglass Houghton and Jacob Houghton, Jr., and their daughter, Lydia, married Alvah Bradish, an artist principally remembered for his portrait and biography of Douglass Houghton. Three of the Douglass brothers, Daniel, Gilbert, and Benjamin, also established themselves in Fredonia; Benjamin's sons, Samuel Townsend Douglass and Silas Hamilton Douglass, established their careers in Michigan, and collections of their papers at the Bentley Historical Library at the University of Michigan are a rich repository of Douglass family history. See J. Lufkin Douglas, *The Douglas Genealogy* (Bath, Me.: Sentinel and Times Publishing, 1890).

   Columbus's father, Christopher Douglass, left Vermont and returned to Connecticut to teach school. His wife, Phoebe, was the daughter of Ivory

Douglass and Phoebe Smith and the granddaughter of William Douglass, Jr., Christopher Douglass's uncle and his mother Lydia's brother. In Springville, New York, as later in Wisconsin, he cleared the land for his farm out of "unbroken wilderness" and served as a judge of the Court of Common Pleas in Erie County. Albert Clayton Beckwith, *History of Walworth County, Wisconsin* (Indianapolis: B. F. Bowen and Co., 1912), 2:1377. For further information on Christopher Douglass see Ruth's entry for February 22, as well as the Douglass genealogy in the appendices.

9. The most eminent of the Douglass cousins was unquestionably Douglass Houghton, whose portrait by his brother-in-law Alvah Bradish hangs in the state capitol. Born in Troy in 1809, raised in Fredonia, and educated at the Rensselaer Institute in Troy, he eventually became very active in the social and political life of Michigan, served a term as mayor of Detroit, was an influential member of the Young Men's Society, helped in the establishment of what would become the University of Michigan, and served prominently as the first state geologist. His observations as geologist and botanist for Schoolcraft's exploring expedition of 1832 and his later exploration of the Upper Peninsula and Isle Royale in 1840 had considerable influence on Michigan politicians, who had high hopes for the mineral resources of the state. When he drowned off the Keweenaw Peninsula in 1845, his death seemed to give him heroic stature in the state. Certainly his influence was felt by his relatives who also established themselves in geology and mining, notably his cousin, C. C. Douglass, and his youngest brother, Jacob Houghton, Jr., born 1827, who was only eighteen when Douglass Houghton died but was also involved in Michigan mining and engineering. Another cousin, Silas Hamilton Douglass, followed in Douglass Houghton's footsteps as a professor at the University of Michigan and worked occasionally as a field geologist for mining concerns.

10. See Bela Hubbard, "A Michigan Geological Expedition in 1837," *Pioneer Collections: Report of the Pioneer Society of the State of Michigan* (Lansing: W. S. George and Co., 1881), 3:189–201; Hubbard, *Memorials of a Half-century in Michigan and the Lake Region* (New York: G. P. Putnam's Sons, 1888); Hubbard, *Lake Superior Journal: Bela Hubbard's Account of the 1840 Houghton Expedition,* ed. Bernard C. Peters (Marquette, Mich.: Northern Michigan University Press, 1983).

11. See Hubbard, "A Michigan Geological Expedition."

12. Douglass Houghton, *Geological Reports of Douglass Houghton, First State Geologist of Michigan, 1837–1845,* ed. George N. Fuller (Lansing: Michigan Historical Commission, 1928).

13. Hubbard, *Lake Superior Journal,* 78. See also Charles W. Penny, *North to Lake Superior: The Journal of Charles W. Penny, 1840,* ed. James L. Carter and Ernest H. Rankin, Sesquicentennial edition (Marquette, Mich.: John M. Longyear Research Library, 1987).

14. Some sense of the sweep of Douglass's duties can be had from his references in a letter he wrote to Abram Sager, Houghton's head of zoology and botany,

on November 19, 1841. He began by claiming, "Having now got fairly seated at my table for the first time since my return from Lake Superior, having had to go to that pleasant place called Saganaw [*sic*] or in other words to the State Salt Works on the Tittapawassie [*sic*] R. from where I returned last night." After describing some of the problems at the salt works, he shifted the subject to the Upper Peninsula: "The district assigned me for examination lies on the Lake Coast between the Ontanagon [*sic*] & Montreal Rivers," and he reported having explored "from 30 to 45 miles back from the Lake." C. C. Douglass to Abram Sager, November 19, 1841, Abram Sager Papers, Bentley Historical Library, Ann Arbor, Michigan.

15. C. C. Douglass to Mr. C[hristopher] Douglass, June 23, 1844, Douglas Worrall Collection, State Archives of Michigan, Lansing.

16. Charles T. Jackson, *Report to the Trustees of Lake Superior Copper Company* (Boston: Beals and Greene, 1845), 391.

17. Jacob Houghton, Jr., *The Mineral Regions of Lake Superior* (Buffalo: O. Steele, 1846), 25–26.

18. Charles Whittlesey, "Two Months in the Copper Region," in *Fugitive Essays* (Hudson, Ohio: Sawyer, Ingersoll, and Co., 1852), 339.

19. Jackson, *Report to the Trustees*, 8.

20. See in particular John Harris Forster, "Early Settlement of the Copper Regions of Lake Superior," *Pioneer Collections: Report of the Pioneer Society of the State of Michigan* (Lansing: Thorp and Godfrey, 1884), 7:181–93; Lewis Marvill, "First Trip by Steam to Lake Superior," *Pioneer Collections: Report of the Pioneer Society of the State of Michigan* (Lansing: W. S. George and Co., 1883), 4:67–69; John H. Pitezel, Journal, Pitezel Collection, Clarke Historical Library, Central Michigan University, Mt. Pleasant; and Pitezel, *Lights and Shades of Missionary Life* (Cincinnati: Western Book Concern, 1857).

21. Beckwith, *History of Walworth County, Wisconsin*, 2:1378; *Portrait and Biographical Record of Walworth and Huron Counties, Wisconsin* (Chicago: Lake Publishing, 1894), 258.

22. *American Biographical History of Eminent and Self-Made Men: Michigan Volume* (Cincinnati: Western Biographical Publishing, 1878), 25–26; *Biographical Record of Houghton, Baraga, and Marquette Counties* (Chicago: Biographical Publishing Co., 1903), 32–33; *History of the Upper Peninsula of Michigan* (Chicago: Western Historical Company, 1883), 85–86.

23. John Harris Forster, "Some Incidents of Pioneer Life in the Upper Peninsula of Michigan," *Pioneer Collections: Report of the Pioneer Society of the State of Michigan* (Lansing: Wynkoop, Hallenbeck, Crawford Co., 1892), 17:341–43.

24. C. C. Douglass to Ransom Shelden, November 20, 1847, Michigan Technological University Archives, Houghton, Michigan.

25. Almon Ernest Parkins, *The Historical Geography of Detroit* (1918; reprint, Port Washington, N.Y.: Kennikat Press, 1970), 170.

26. Ibid., 189; Harriet Martineau, *Society in America* (London, 1837; reprint, New York: AMS Press, 1966), 1:314.
27. George B. Catlin, *A Brief History of Detroit in the Golden Days of '49* (Detroit: Detroit Savings Bank, 1921), 6.
28. Letter written by "Helen," 1847, Clarke Historical Library, Central Michigan University, 2.
29. Martineau, *Society in America*, 1:314.
30. Fredrika Bremer, *The Homes of the New World: Impressions of America,* trans. Mary Howitt (1853; reprint, New York: Johnson Reprint Corporation, 1968), 1:597–98.
31. Martineau, *Society in America*, 1:316.
32. Friend Palmer, *Early Days in Detroit* (Detroit: Hunt and Jones, 1906), 225.
33. Ibid., 288.
34. Catlin, *A Brief History of Detroit*, 29.
35 George B. Catlin, "Oliver Newberry," *Michigan History* 18 (winter 1934): 5.
36. Ibid., 10.
37. Ibid., 16.
38. Ibid., 21.
39. James H. Wellings, *Directory of the City of Detroit and Register of Michigan for the Year 1846* (Detroit: A. S. Williams, 1846), 159.
40. *The Detroit Advertiser*, August 11, 1848, p. 1.
41. Bremer, *The Homes of the New World*, 1:599–600.
42. Martineau, *Society in America,* 1:338.
43. Bremer, *The Homes of the New World*, 1:628.
44. Dunlop, *Sixty Miles from Contentment*, 3.
45. Caroline Kirkland, *Western Clearings* (New York: Putnam, 1845), vi.
46. Dunlop, *Sixty Miles from Contentment*, 3.
47. Martineau, *Society in America,* 1:350.
48. William Cullen Bryant, *The Letters of William Cullen Bryant, 1836–1849*, ed. William Cullen Bryant II and Thomas G. Voss (New York: Fordham University Press, 1977), 2:446.
49. Bremer, *The Homes of the New World*, 1:605–06.
50. Bryant, *Letters*, 2:445.
51. Bremer, *The Homes of the New World*, 1:614.
52. Beckwith, *History of Walworth County, Wisconsin*, 2:377.
53. Martineau, *Society in America*, 1:357–58.
54. Bremer, *The Homes of the New World,* 1:627.
55. Ibid., 1:629.
56. [Andrew Rundel], "A Copper Prospector in 1846," ed. Alice E. Smith, *Michigan History* 33, no. 2 (June 1949): 143.
57. Bryant, *Letters*, 2:465.
58. Ibid., 2:444.
59. Charles Lanman, *A Summer in the Wilderness Embracing a Canoe Voyage up the Mississippi and around Lake Superior* (New York: D. Appleton and Company, 1847), 165.

60. Bryant, *Letters*, 2:453.
61. Ibid., 2:464.
62. *Journal of a Trip to Michigan, 1848*, MSS JJ-75, Clarke Historical Library, Central Michigan University, Mt. Pleasant, 12.
63. Bryant, *Letters*, 2:455.
64. Ibid., 2:456.
65. Lanman, *Summer in the Wilderness*, 157.
66. Bryant, *Letters*, 2:454.
67. J. Lang Cassels, *Geological and Mineralogical Report upon the Mineral Lands on Isle Royale, Lake Superior, Belonging to the Isle Royale & Ohio Mining Company* (Cleveland: Smead and Cowles, 1846), 4, 5.
68. Ibid., 5, 6.
69. Leander Ransom to Elisha Whittlesey, January 6, 1847, Elisha Whittlesey Papers, Western Reserve Historical Society, Cleveland, 1, 3–4.
70. *Charter and By-Laws of the Siskowit Mining Company of Michigan, together with the Treasurer's Report, &c. up to January 1, 1850* (Philadelphia: John Clarke, 1850), appendix, pp. 2, 4.
71. Charles Whittlesey, "Report of Charles Whittlesey, Agent, to the President and Directors, Siskowit Mining Company, May 25, 1848," *American Mining Journal and Rail Road Gazette* (June 21, 1848): n.p.
72. Horace Greeley, "Lake Superior—Copper Mining—The 'Cliff.'" *American Mining Journal and Railroad Gazette 2* (1848/1849): 58.
73. Ibid.
74. Senate, *Report on the Geological and Mineralogical Survey of the Mineral Lands of the United States in the State of Michigan*, by Charles T. Jackson, 31st Cong., 1st sess., 1849–50, S. Doc. 1, pt. 3, p. 419.
75. Ibid., 427.
76. Lawrence Frederick Rakestraw, *Historic Mining on Isle Royale* (Houghton: Isle Royale Natural History Association in cooperation with the National Park Service, 1965), 3.
77. *Charter*, 11.
78. Alfred C. Lane, "Part I: Isle Royale," in *The Upper Peninsula, 1893–1897, Volume 6*. (Lansing: Robert Smith Printing, 1898), 11.
79. A. Myers, Transcript of Journey to Siskowit Mine in 1851 by A. Myers, Historical Society of Pennsylvania, AM 448, August 13 entry and clipping.
80. Lane, "Part I: Isle Royale," 11.
81. J. W. Foster and J. D. Whitney, *Report on the Geology and Topography of the Lake Superior Land District in the State of Michigan, Part I. Copperlands* (Washington: Printed for the House of Representatives, 1850–51), 142.
82. Rakestraw, *Historic Mining on Isle Royale*, 6.
83. Foster and Whitney, *Report on the Geology and Topography . . .*, 171.
84. *Charter*, 11.
85. Foster and Whitney, *Report on the Geology and Topography . . .*, 143, 144.
86. Myers, Journal entry for August 15, 1851.

87. Lanman, *Summer in the Wilderness*, 128, 129–30.

88. Foster and Whitney, *Report on the Geology and Topography . . .* , 81–82.

89. *Report on the Geological and Mineralogical Survey*, 428–29.

90. Cornelius Shaw, Diary, 1847, Bentley Historical Library, University of Michigan, Ann Arbor; see entries by date.

91. Myers, Journal entries, August 14 and 15, 1851.

92. The dangers of isolation were real and sometimes tragic, as the well-known story of Charlie and Angelique Mott shows. Hired by Cyrus Mendenhall to occupy a mining site on the island over the winter, the Motts were promised supplies when they went to Isle Royale on July 1, 1845, but none were delivered, possibly through neglect on Mendenhall's part. The couple were stranded on the island with insufficient provisions and endured starvation. When Charlie died in mid-winter, Angelique left his body in the cabin and moved into an outbuilding where she was able to snare snowshoe hares using a trap woven from strands of her hair. She survived on these meager provisions until spring, when shipping opened and supplies finally were delivered. It was a story that C. C. Douglass probably knew well, since, according to Angelique Mott, she and Charlie went, "on their invitation," with "Mr. Douglas [*sic*], Mr. Barnard and some other 'big bugs' from Detroit" to Isle Royale, where Angelique's discovery of "a piece of mass copper" encouraged them to hire the Motts to winter over on the island. (Ralph D. Williams, *The Honorable Peter White* [Cleveland: Penton Publishing Co., 1907], 149–52.) Ruth Douglass visited Charlie Mott's grave in the Siskowit graveyard during her first months on the island.

Another incident of this kind occurred after the mining companies had made an effort to provide for their employees, and an exceptionally hard winter devastated delivery of supplies and forced people to fend for themselves. In 1851, when the Siskowit Mine was the only one still operating on the island, the situation became grave for the community gathered near the mine. As Jane Masters later recalled it,

> In 1852 navigation opened so late that the last morsel of meat was eaten. For six weeks all of us had to subsist on bread and syrup and so weak did the men become from this scant nourishment that the mine was closed. Driven to desperation, twenty men determined to reach Fort William, and an improvised boat and sleigh were skidded across the ice. . . . [at Fort William] no meat could be furnished. A settler came to their rescue with an offer to slaughter a cow and this was hastily accepted. The meat was placed in the boat and to protect it, balsam boughs were spread upon it. By the time the men reached the island, the balsam had penetrated the meat and our joy was again turned to sorrow. A few days later a boat appeared laden with provisions, but we remained on the island only long enough to board a southbound boat to Keweenaw. ("Recollections of an Old Copper Country Resident," *The Calumet News*, March 17, 1913)

Drawing of C. C. Douglass by Bela Hubbard. (Courtesy of the Bentley Historical Library.)

Portrait of Christopher Douglass. (Courtesy of the State Historical Society of Wisconsin, WHi(X3)50436.)

Drawing of C. L. Douglass's farm in Wisconsin. (Courtesy of the State Historical Society of Wisconsin, WHi(X3)50435.)

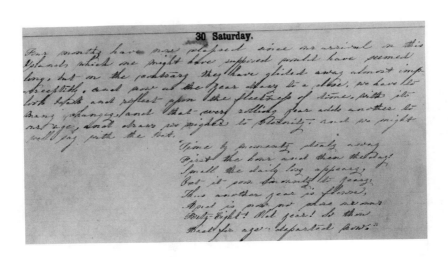

Final entry of Ruth Douglass's journal. (Courtesy of the Clarke Historical Library.)

Lithograph of Cliff Mine, 1849. (Courtesy of the Bentley Historical Library.)

Lithograph of Columnar Trap [Scovill Point], Isle Royale, from Foster and Whitney. (Courtesy of the Bentley Historical Library.)

Photograph of surviving Siskowit Mine building, 1868. (Courtesy of the Bentley Historical Library.)

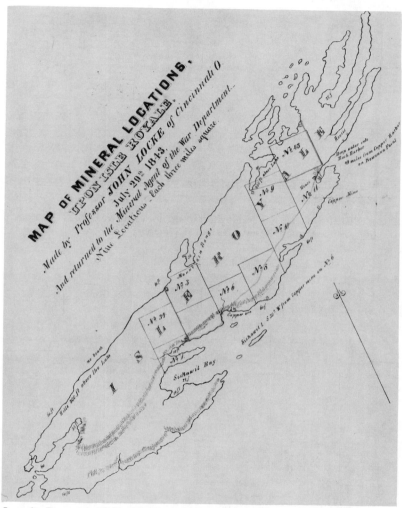

Leander Ransom's 1847 additions to John Locke's 1843 map of Isle Royale & Ohio holdings on Isle Royale. (Courtesy of the Western Reserve Historical Society.)

Share of Isle Royale & Ohio Mining Company stock held by Elisha Whittlesey. (Courtesy of the Western Reserve Historical Society.)

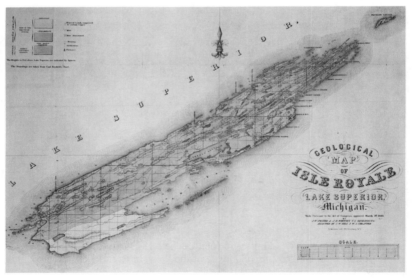

Geological map of Isle Royale, 1848. (Courtesy of the Bentley Historical Library.)

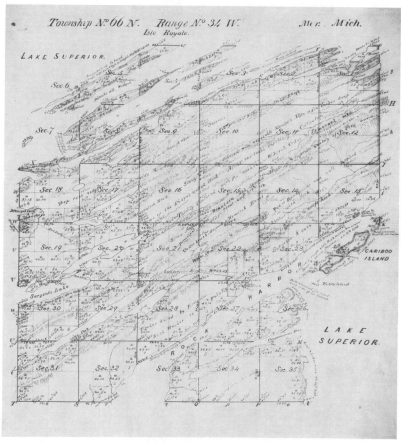

Section map of Isle Royale by William Ives. (Courtesy of the Bentley Historical Library.)

Drawing of Douglass Houghton Mine location. (Courtesy of the Burton Historical Collection.)

Lydia S. Douglass, second wife Columbus C. Douglass, c. 1867–68 (From the private collection of Lloyd Tucker Wescoat. Reprinted with permission.)

Columbus C. Douglass, c. 1867–68. (From the private collection of Lloyd Tucker Wescoat. Reprinted with permission.)

Katharine L. Douglass, daughter of Lydia and Columbus C. Douglass, c. 1867–68. (From the private collection of Lloyd Tucker Wescoat. Reprinted with permission.)

Courtney C. Douglass, son of Lydia and Columbus C. Douglass, c. 1867–68. (From the private collection of Lloyd Tucker Wescoat. Reprinted with permission.)

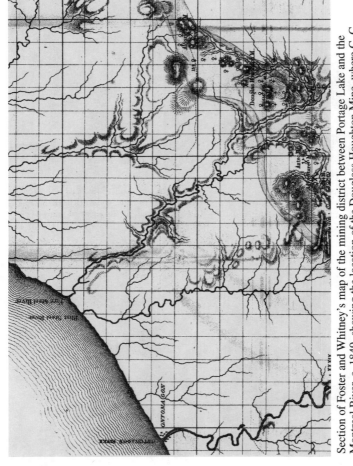

Section of Foster and Whitney's map of the mining district between Portage Lake and the Montreal River, c. 1849, showing the location of the Douglass Houghton Mine, where C. C. and Ruth Douglass lived during 1849–50, in relation to Ontonagon, where Ruth died in June 1850. (From J. W. Foster and J. D. Whitney, *Report on the Geology and Topography of a Portion of the Lake Superior Land District in the State of Michigan. Part I. Copperlands.* Washington: Printed for the House of Representatives, 1850–51.)

The Journal of
Ruth Edgerton Douglass

January

MRS. C. C. DOUGLASS, DETROIT, MICHIGAN, JAN. 1ST 1848

Mr Douglass brought in this Book to day and presented it to me, saying, as we should probably be moving about some the coming year it would be well to keep a journal of our migrations. I very willingly acceded to this wish, but shall not attempt to carry out the design of the Author, by keeping a regular daily journal but will endeavor to record incidents as they may occur.

1 SATURDAY

A very rainy day. Received a few calls in Detroit. I think it is becoming fashionable to have wet New Year's, as this is the third one in succession that it has been very rainy. The gentlemen are talking of adopting some other day, for calling upon the Ladies, it being rather unpleasant wading about in the rain and mud. The departure of the old year, and the commencement of the new, is attended, by many serious reflections. There is much truth in the following simple lines, which describe my feelings better than I can speak them myself.

> "Forty-Eight! The year's begun!
> Hail'd by many! known to none
> Gladsome bells, with merry peal,
> Thine auspicious birth reveal;
> Who may hear thy parting knell,
> <u>God, and he alone can tell.</u>"[1]

3 MONDAY

We are making preparations now to go to Wisconsin to spend the remainder of the Winter. We had intended to start to day, but as we were not quite ready we have concluded to postpone our journey for one week. It being necessary to leave here on Monday, in order to intercept the Stage at Chicago.

4 TUESDAY

The weather is pleasant overhead, but it is difficult getting about much, the mud has frozen so suddenly that the roads are unaccountably rough. I dread our intended journey through the country, as we shall be obliged to travel most of the way, (at least from Kalamazoo,) in Stage.

5 WEDNESDAY

Mr. Douglass has gone to Mt. Clemens to day.[2] The roads are so bad he was oblidged to go on horse-back, if he had gone with a waggon I should have accompanied him. I expect him back to morrow.

6 THURSDAY

Spent the afternoon at Samuel's, waited for C. C. to come until 9. o'clock, then concluding he would not be along to night. Samuel came down with me.[3] I feel quite uneasy about him, fearing he may be sick, as he had a very bad cold when he left home.

7 FRIDAY

My fears about C. C. were too true, he returned this Evening quite unwell, scarcely able to speak above a whisper he is so hoarse, says he was down sick yesterday. he coughs very bad.

8 SATURDAY

The Weather is very cold, I hope it will change before Monday, I have my boxes all packed and in readiness. It is necessary to be 'all ready' to day, as the cars leave so early in the morning, that I shall not have any time for preparation then.

10 MONDAY

Left Detroit for Walworth, Walworth Co., Wisconsin[4] at 8. o'clock A.M. in cars, arrived at Kalamazoo[5] at 11. P.M., supped, took stage and rode all night. Weather <u>very</u> cold.

11 TUESDAY

Stopt at Three Rivers & breakfasted, then proceeded on in stage, arrived at Niles about 8. P.M., took supper, rode all night.[6] Weather continues very cold.

12 WEDNESDAY

Arrived at Michigan City early in the morning. breakfasted and proceeded on our way to Chicago, where we arrived at 10. in the evening, quite fatigued and retired to rest. Weather more moderate, Michigan City is a very sandy desolate looking place, Chicago a fine flourishing City.[7]

13 THURSDAY

Left Chicago in the morning at 8 o'clock, took a post coach for Walworth, most of the way through oak openings and over prairies. arrived at Bangs half way house at 9 in the evening,[8] stopt through the night. Weather very moderate, some rain.

14 FRIDAY

After breakfast proceeded on our journey. Most of to days ride through a fine section of country, arrived at our place of destination on Big Foot prairie about sun set.[9] about tired of stage riding in Winter, and quite happy to get to our journey's end.

15 SATURDAY

After a good nights rest, felt quite refreshed, took a ride round the farm much pleased with the Prairie and situation of the farm. We were very cordially received by all the family on our arrival here. Having never seen Mr. Douglass Parents, Brothers, nor Sisters except Lavelette & Josiphene before.[10]

17 MONDAY

There being only weekly mail for this place, and as to day is the day of the week it passes East-ward, I shall write home that our Friends may know of our safe arrival at this our place of destination. They with me looked upon a journey through the Country in winter as almost insurmountable. There is always more or less fatigue experienced in journeying particularly when one travels nights, although this was performed more easily than I anticipated. Saw a number of my new relations yesterday and the day before. Brothers and Sisters many more than I can boast in our own family.[11] There were several of them home to supper yesterday that reside a few miles distant.

22 SATURDAY

We have been to pay a visit to Mr. Douglass eldest Brother to day.[12] He resides on a farm about seven miles from this, lying in the State of Illinois. had a very pleasant visit, and ride. We passed through some beautiful oak openings,[13] and ascended a hill (which bears the appellation of Quality Hill) from which we had a delightful view of the Prairie.[14]

24 MONDAY

The weather is now very pleasant, there is no snow on the ground and the roads are dry as in Summer. Mr Douglass, Josiphene and myself have just returned from a walk. We went up into the openings and followed a path leading to the head of Geneva Lake.[15] After wandering about through these beautiful openings for some distance we came to a spring of clear water, from which the inhabitants for some distance around used to draw—here we saw the recent foot-prints of a wolf in the sand[16]—The remains of an old building nearly gone to decay was to be seen near the Spring. becoming some-what fatigued, we concluded to postpone our walk to the Lake, and take a view of it from a hill near by. We crossed the trail of the celebrated Black Hawk[17] and ascended the hill from which we had a fine view of the Lake and Prairie. This hill forms the dividing rige between the waters of the Fox and Rock Rivers.[18]

February

1 TUESDAY

This morning is one of those particularly clear and pleasant ones when a person can see about as far as could be consistently wished some seven or eight miles. The Prairie bears every resemblance to an old settled country, and I can hardly believe that the first settlement was made upon it in '38. On every side you turn your eye you behold large cultivated fields neatly fenced, also good buildings as one sees in passing through almost any farming district, even in the State of New York.

The Prairie is bounded on the East, West, & North by undulating ground covered with scattering oak trees, having wide scraggy tops and not tall, strikingly resemble apple trees—I often look out upon this beautiful border and exclaim what a fine orchard, it must have been a long time growing, and I find it very difficult to divest myself of the conviction that they are indeed Apple trees.

7 MONDAY

Mr. Douglass started for Indianapolis this Evening, and I am to remain here during his abscence, he thinks he will be back in three or four weeks, he will be obliged to travel in the stage nearly or quite all the way, had there been other modes of conveyance, I would have accompanied him.

10 THURSDAY

This has been a long week to me, but I have the consolation of thinking that tomorrow is mail day, as we have mail only once a week I look forward to the day with much anxiety.

11 FRIDAY

The mail came in, in good season to day, and Lyda[19] and I rode up to the Post Office in the stage, and walked home, the distance is over a mile, we had a very pleasant walk, the weather is delightful, it seems so much like Spring. I received two letters, one from Mr. Douglass from Chicago, and one from Sister.[20]

14 MONDAY

A very pleasant morning, The Beaux, and Belles, of Walworth are on the move to attend a ride and Ball at Jefferson Prairie,[21] some fourteen miles distant. I believe they are intending to start immediately after dinner, and return tomorrow morning. As there is no snow, they will have the pleasure of going in wagons.

15 TUESDAY

Eleven A.M. The young people have just returned, Lavelette looks as though he had not slept in a week. said they had a very large and pleasant party.

18 FRIDAY

The wheeling is not as good as it was last week, consequently the mail did not arrive to day, but I shall look for it early tomorrow morning. The roads here are so level that one is able to see a great distance, and I have almost strained my eyes to day, thinking to see the stage coming, I feel very anxious to hear from C. C. and from home.

19 SATURDAY

This morning is quite rainy but the mail came in at an early hour, and I have just finished reading and re-reading my letters. I received one from Sister informing me of the good health of all our friends and family, but that there is at present a great deal of sickness in the City, a disease called the 'spotted fever' having made its appearance in a malignant form, which is sweeping off many to a sudden and early death,[22] C.C. wrote me from La porte Indiana, (where he was detained two days, the stage running from thence only to Indianapolis only tri-weekly,) he thinks he shall go from Indianapolis to Cincinatti and from there to Detroit, if so, I think it will be more than four weeks before he gets round home.

22 TUESDAY

This day is celebrated as the birth day of General George Washington, who has been very justly styled "The Father of our Country." This makes the one hundredth and sixteenth anniversary. There is no attempt made in this place to pay any honor to the day. It is also a day on record in our family, being the Sixty first Anniversary of Father Douglass birthday. who, though not the Father of his Country is the Father of ten children. Most of them are now settled near him. He has just given me a sketch of his emigrations from his boyhood up to the present time, together with the hardships and privations incidental to a settlement in a new country.

Being born as on this day, in the year 1787, in New-London, Connecticut, he removed with his Parents when a small Boy to Rutland Vermont, while the Country was yet new. here he remained with his Parents on a farm, until he married and removed from thence in the year 1809, to the western part of the State of New York, Town of Concord, Erie County, (going the whole distance with an Ox team,) where he commenced the world for himself, by clearing up a farm on the banks of the Cattaraugus Creek. here they endured privations, and hardships of which we of the present day, know but little, and would appear to us as almost incredible. Buffalo, Rochester, and other places, now flourishing Cities then contained only a few log cabins.

Remained here until the Country became somewhat thickly settled around him, and having a predilection for a life in a new Country, visited Michigan in 1825, being much pleased with this then new Country.

Purchased a farm near Mt. Clemens, Macomb County, on which he removed with his family in the fall of '27, this proved to be a very unhealthy place, the <u>whole</u> family suffering severely from the effects of ague and fever, and may well be termed the 'plague of Michigan.' Michigan was then a territory comprising within its jurisdiction what is now, Michigan, Wisconsin, and Iowa, having a population of 27,000 inhabitants.

The Black Hawk war being terminated, and the western Prairies laid open to the pioneer, he determined to go still fa[r]ther on in hopes of finding the promised land, and as the Cry then was 'Westward ho!' he bent his course in '37 towards Northern Illinois, where he made a temporary home, for one year, (at Elk Grove 18 miles North West of Chicago,) in order to make choice of a more permanent one, while stopping here the family suffered much from sickness.

Emigration increasing at this time so fast as to render the consumption of provisions greater than the production, the result of which was, exorbitant prices for all kinds of provisions, such as $30.00 a barrel for pork and $20 for flour, having it to carry from Chicago that being their nearest market, after looking about and surveying the country he settled on this beautiful prairie. The first winter they passed here there was but one other family on the prairie.

And now after spending so much of his life on the frontier He says he would rather go west than East.

March

9 THURSDAY

Josiphene and I went up to see Mrs. Huff this morning,[23] found the walking quite rough. After returning home, I went over to Roxanna's and was quite surprised to find little Calla sick in bed.[24] Roxanna said she came home from school yesterday afternoon saying she felt very bad and sick, and that she continued quite sick having a high fever so that she and the Doctor were up with her all night. She appears quite alarmed about her. We hope she may recover soon.

10 FRIDAY

The day is very pleasant and Spring like. we think Caroline a little better, though still dangerously ill. I watched all the afternoon for the stage, but looked in vain until 5. P.M. Esther[25] & Josiphene went up to a high window and returned saying they saw a Black Bear moving this way on the Chicago road. it soon rolled up to the door, and to my joy out stepped C. C. These five weeks have seemed long to me on account of his abscence. He brings me some news, and presents, also some wedding cake having attended the wedding of his friend Bella on the 2nd Inst.[26] The girls might well compare the Stage to a Bear, as it has a long top covered with black oil cloth.

11 SATURDAY

Little Caroline died this Morning about ten o'clock. She was struck with death at 2. A.M. and remained senseless afterwards strugling with death, it was an affecting scene to witness. One might well say of her—

> A lovely flower
> Cut down and withered in an hour[27]

The disease which carried her away was thought to be the Spotted or Congestive fever. She was eight years old, and a very engaging Child. she is to be burried tomorrow.

April

15 SATURDAY

The mail arrived early this morning, and C. C. has received a note from Mr. Bell the P.M.[28] saying he learned from the driver that there was a steam-Boat passed up to Chicago yesterday, which would leave for Buffalo, Monday morning. We are now making preparations to leave here early tomorrow morning in order to intercept the Steamer at Southport on Monday.[29]

17 MONDAY

Southport,—Monday morning. We arrived here about sun-set last Evening and learned much to our disappointment that the Steamer which had passed, amounted to only two Propellers, they being the only boats which were able to get through the ice at the Straights of Mackinaw.[30] We shall probably wait here two or three days and then if no boat come, take stage to Chicago, and thence home through the country.

We found beautiful wheeling all the way from Walworth until within three miles of this village, the roads very badly cut up, the dust flew as in summer we were completely covered when we arrived here.

We walked down to the Lake and out to the end of the pier, and gazed upon its broad expanse of water, but no sail or smoke appeared to greet our eyes. The Propeller Manhattan came up about sunset bound for Detroit. We thought quite seriously of going on board, but knowing her to be an old boat, and not liking the black clouds which appeared in the N. E. concluded to take the Princeton which was expected in the morning.[31]

18 TUESDAY

We were awakened this morning by the peltings of a violent storm against the windows. The wind blew furiously from the North-East accompanied with hail and snow. The appearance of the Lake was truly frightful—the waves rolled and dashed madly over the high piers, sweeping away much valuable property. About daybreak a Boat was seen, (supposed to be the Princeton) which being unable to make head way against the storm turned back towards Chicago. A few hours after another Boat was seen thought to be 4 or 5 miles distant from this place apparently laboring hard, and nearly abandoned to the fury of the waves—as at one time she appeared to be heading the storm, then lying in the trough of the seas, sometimes gliding before it without a sign of sail, and finally disappeared causing many apprehensions for her safety. The storm continued to rage violently, until about 3 P.M. when it began to abate. This storm appeared to me so frightful that I remarked I never wished to go out on the Lake again, that I prefered returning home by land.[32]

19 WEDNESDAY

Considering it useless to wait longer at Southport, we took stage for Chicago about 10 A.M. intending to return home by land. There were twelve passengers in the vehicle, 3 or 4 of whom were on the unfortunate Manhattan when she went ashore near Racine[33] yesterday, we learn by them, that the propeller had nearly reached Manitou Islands[34] when she was driven back by the Storm. It is fortunate for us that we did not go on board of her. The storm of yesterday had made the road almost impassable. We moved along very slowly through the mud, and arrived at Little Fort[35]—15 miles from Southport about 3 P.M. stopped for dinner and started again with fresh horses, but had not proceeded but a short distance when the horses refused to go, and upset the stage, in a deep place. The men took me out, and carried me on to a dry place, and after unloading all the baggage raised the Stage with levers. Reloaded again and moved along but soon the cry was heard, from the driver 'You must get out', then the men would all unload, and leave me to ride through the mud alone.

20 THURSDAY

Sherman House, Chicago-3. P.M.[36] We arrived about daybreak this morn after a wearisome ride all night, and I must say that if this is any thing of a sample of stage riding in Wisconsin those are to be pitied that have to perform more extended journeys. After rising from a few hours of refreshing sleep, felt quite refreshed and highly gratified to learn, the steamer Michigan had arrived.[37] She leaves for Detroit tomorrow. We shall return on her. Uncle Oliver came up on the Michigan, and came with Uncle Walter up to see us this morning.[38] This morning we had a fine view of the City— from the observatory of this building, after which Uncle Walter took me in his carriage all about the town, pointing out all the 'Lions' of which Chicago boasts[39] and then up to his garden which is beautiful. Hyacinths, violets, and Daffodils, and many other spring flowers all in bloom. I have a beautiful bouquet of them. Mr. Clark called upon me just now. I saw a number of familiar looking faces at the table, and I now begin to feel as though I was getting near home.

21 FRIDAY

I was quite impatient for the Boat to depart this morning, but she did not get ready to leave until near evening. As we moved up the Lake it appeared to me as if we were ascending a hill, Chicago looked so low, we stayed out on deck, (the weather being quite like Summer here) until we lost sight of the City. The reflection of the setting Sun added beauty to the view. Uncle Oliver returns home with us. Uncle Walter came down to see us depart, and brought me a beautiful bouquet from his own garden to take home.

There is a family on board consisting of a Lady and six children, that were wrecked on a vessel in the gale of Tuesday. She informed me they were driven by the wind from near Manitou Islands down below the piers in Chicago. one man was blown off and drowned, and she with her children were swimming about in the Cabin nearly strangled, and expecting to be drowned every moment. I feel much sympathy for this Lady, as she is to all appearance an excellent woman.

22 SATURDAY

We find ourselves in Milwaukie this morning, and as the Boat is to remain here most of the day we shall have an opportunity to see something of the City.

After breakfast we took a ramble through the Town and up to the high lands to the East of it where we had a fine view of the City and Harbor, Milwaukie is pleasantly situated on a River of the same name, and contains many beautiful buildings, a large number of which are of yellow brick which give them a fine appearance. It is styled one of the new Cities of the West and now contains a population of some 17,000 inhabitants.[40]

May

9 TUESDAY

Great Fire in Detroit.[41] C. C. Douglass left Detroit for Lake Superior at 10 A.M.[42] A visit from Sister Atwood.[43] Martha Porter married at 11 A.M.[44]

27 SATURDAY

I have been quite unwell all day and am about fit to be called sick. Fanny and Ann started for Buffalo on the Michigan this Evening.[45] I intended to have gone down to the Boat with them but was not able to go. I think they will have a pleasant trip.

June

3 SATURDAY

The Michigan arrived about 5. P.M. bringing up Uncle H- & Aunt Ruth, Fanny and Ann, together with a nice basket of Cincinnati strawberries the first I have seen this year.[46] Aunt Ruth says they left home on Tuesday, came through very quick I think, stopping nearly two days in Buffalo in the time. She stood the journey remarkably well.

6 TUESDAY

Aunt Ruth & Uncle H- left for Ann Arbor in the cars this morning to visit a Sister of his, that resides a short distance from there. They intend to return to us in two or three days.

7 WEDNESDAY

Simeon Draper died this afternoon at half past 2. o'clock at Mrs. Felker's.[47] he was taken sick last Friday. his disease was thought to be the spotted fever. He was a very fine young man, and highly esteemed by all who knew him.

8 THURSDAY

Mrs. Draper and her eldest Son arrived from Rochester this morning. They received the tidings of his death by Telegraph at Cleaveland. They return with his remains to Rochester, N.Y., this evening.

Fanny and I have just been down to see Henry White, he is lying very low, and I am afraid will never be any better.

Mrs. Shepherd called this morning all ready to start on a pleasure trip to New York by way of the falls of Niagra, Montreal &c.[48]

9 FRIDAY

The afternoon has been rainy. Our friends returned from Ann Arbor this Evening, quite pleased with their excursion.

10 SATURDAY

The day has been very pleasant. Mother, Aunt Ruth, Fanny and Oliver have been out riding, giving Aunt an opportunity to see something of the Town and surrounding Country.[49]

12 MONDAY

I looked for C. C. yesterday until the Detroit arrived without him. The time he set that he should be back has now passed, and it will be five weeks tomorrow since he left.

14 WEDNESDAY

C. C. Douglass returned from Lake Superior to Detroit, came from Mackinaw on Steamer Nile.[50] Arrived home in the morning. Walked with me in the evening up to see Uncle Benjamin, found him very low.[51]

15 THURSDAY

C. C. is consoling himself this morning that he is at home, for if he had waited for the Detroit he would have been obliged to remain at the Soo a week, the Detroit having left for Detroit, about 3 hours before his arrival, he with others, then took a small boat to Mackinaw, where he had the good fortune to meet the Nile on which he came down.[52]

16 FRIDAY

Uncle Benjamin Douglass departed this life at 2. P.M. He dropt away very suddenly with a disease of the Heart.

17 SATURDAY

Burried at half past six in Elmwood Cemetary. Attended his funeral from his residence on Jefferson Avenue, Detroit Michigan.

August

1 TUESDAY

When Mr Douglass came up to tea, he said he had received a letter from the Ohio and Isle Royale mining Co.[53] with the proposition to go to Isle

Royale Lake Superior to establish smelting works, and Ruth will you go with me? I replied. Oui Monsieur, he then remarked that although he had led something of a back woods life, and was ready to go to almost any place, but the idea of being banished to a desolate island was something that had not entered his head.

2 WEDNESDAY

There is nothing said about going to Isle Royale to day, I abstain from mentioning it in hopes it may blow over.

3 THURSDAY

They seem determined to prevail on C. C. to go to Isle Royale, as one of the directors of the Company (Mr. Giddings[54]) has come up from Cleaveland to day to see if he will go.

17 THURSDAY

Sailed from Detroit about 12. P.M., bound for Isle Royale Lake Superior, on Steamer Michigan.[55] The weather being pleasant, and the moon shining almost as bright as the Sun, we passed over the 'St. Clair flats' without any detention before day-break.[56]

18 FRIDAY

At sunrise found ourselves at Algonac a small town on the St. Clair River,[57] the boat stopt for wood, and took on four gents & ladies going to the Sault for a pleasure trip. Passed Newport (without stopping) a small town situated at the mouth of the Bell River,[58] the residence of the steamboats Yards. About an hour after leaving Newport passed Palmer, the county seat of St. Clair County situated on a high bank at the mouth of Pine River.[59] Arrived at Black River at 2. P.M., a place noted for its excellency and quantity of Pine lumber, Port Sarnia lying on the Canada shore directly opposite.[60] One mile above, passed Fort Gratiot at the entrance of Lake Huron,[61] at this place the St. Clair River is contracted into one half of its average width below, having a current of 7 miles an hour. passed Point aux Barques and crossed Saginaw Bay during the night.[62]

19 SATURDAY

Arrived at Mackinaw about sun set, having had fine weather & a very pleasant trip, went out for a walk, made a call upon Mrs. Graveret,[63] returned to the boat. wrote a letter home, retired to rest, and about 10. P.M.

set sail for Sault de Ste Marie where we arrived on Sunday the 20th at 3.
P.M. During the day passed Thunder bay islands a place fast becoming celebrated for its white fisheries.[64] Government established a light house at
this place many years since. Called at Presque Ile for wood, being the only
eligible wooding place on Lake Huron, it affords a safe and commodious
harbor.[65]

21 MONDAY

At the Sault de Ste Marie, Van Anden's Hotel.[66] Received calls from Mrs.
Col. McNair, Mrs. Dr. Patterson, Mrs. McKnight & Col. McNair &
Daughter, in the Morning.[67] In the evening went out riding, and saw some
very large masses of pure native Copper unladen from Propeller
Independence.[68] I suppose we shall be detained here several days, as the
Propeller only came down last night and will not go up again until the last
of the week, or until after the arrival of the Detroit.

22 TUESDAY

In the Morning walked down to the wharf to see the Michigan take its
departure, wished that there was a passage around the Falls of St Marie so
that she might have brought us up Lake Superior.[69] Mr. Douglass has been
attending the land sale to day, and I have been reading "The Bachelor of
the Albany."[70]

23 WEDNESDAY

This must pass for a rainy day, from my chamber window at Van Andens,
I have a fine view of the rapids. The Indians are very busy fishing, they go
out quite into the rapids in bark canoes to fish. Walked up to the Fort[71] in
the evening and returned a number of calls.

24 THURSDAY

All are looking anxiously for the Steamer Detroit this morning as the
Propeller will not leave until after her arrival, she did not however arrive
till about sun-set. She brought a number of passengers to go up Lake
Superior, among them were Horrace Greely editor of the New York
Tribune,[72] going as far as Eagle Harbor, and Mr. Watson, and Johnson, mer-
chants of Detroit, going up to La Point to attend the Indian payments.[73]

25 FRIDAY

Rather an unfavorable looking morning for going out upon Lake Superior,
clears away about noon, and is looking pleasant. Went on board the

Propeller directly after tea, there were a large load of passengers & freight. Being no wharf, we were obliged to go out for some distance on a scow, and then climb up a ladder, to get on board of the Propeller. We set sail about mid-night.

26 SATURDAY

This morning finds us sailing on the broad blue waters of Lake Superior, at the rate of about 5 or 6 miles per hour. We are quite out of sight of land.

28 MONDAY

Yesterday morning saw schooner Napoleon[74] off Copper Harbor. the fog was so dense we were unable to see that place, we passed on to Eagle Harbor[75] where we arrived about 10. A.M. stopt about two hours. Horrace Greely of New York came up with us and stopt here. they have a wharf at this place, and the only one I saw anywheres on the whole trip long enough to admit of the Propeller coming along side. stop. I will except the one at La Point, but I think these are the only two on Lake Superior. the boat stopt for a short time at, or near, Eagle River at this place they have to go out for a long distance in a small boat, we intended to go directly from this place to Isle Royale, but the wind changed and we proceeded direct to La Point, where we arrived on Monday about noon, we passed the Apostles Islands near by, there were some 2 or 3 thousand Indians assembled to receive their yearly payments. La Point is quite a pretty little town, it belongs to the group of Apostle Islands.[76] Mr. Douglass & myself were invited up to spend the afternoon at Dr. Livermores the Indian Agent at this place.[77] We went, and returned to the Propeller in the eve—when we set sail for Isle Royale.

29 TUESDAY

This morning found us abreast of Porcupine Mountains a high range of hills, varying from five hundred to fourteen hundred feet above the level of Lake Superior. This range of mountains has its easterly terminus near the Lake coast and a little West of Iron River, they extend south westerly beyond the limit of the state of Michigan into the State of Wisconsin. We next came to the Ontonogan River[78] where we landed some passengers and freight. This is one of the largest streams on the south shore of Lake Superior, and is said to pass through a rich mineral district. I did not go on shore, but the view from the boat was pleasant, the banks being somewhat elevated, from this we went to Ransom City, Rock Harbor, Isle Royale, our course being a few degrees East of North.

30 WEDNESDAY

Arrived on the Royal Isle at 8 in the Morning. looks very pleasant. The inhabitants hoisted their flag and fired salutes on our arrival. On the whole our trip has been a very pleasant one.

When I arose in the morning we were in sight of the Island about 15 miles west of our place of destination, keeping near the shore we had a fine view of the coast with its bold rocky cliffs small bays and fine harbors. The view thus obtained of the Island was any thing but a favorable one for me at least, as there was nothing to be seen but barren rocks and a small growth of evergreen and birch timber. as my eyes had not the gift of magnifying every little seam in the rocks into a large vein of Copper. This being the sole inducement for people to settle in this remote region. As we entered Rock Harbor I was happily disappointed at the appearance of our temporary home.

31 THURSDAY

Very busy to day house cleaning, and making an effort to get settled in our new log Cabin, which I find more pleasantly situated and comfortable than I anticipated, the house being very large and quite convenient, having eight large rooms on the first floor, also commodious chambers. 'Ransom City' (for such it has been christened) can also boast of several other buildings such as a Store, Labratory, Office and storehouse attached, Furnace & Blacksmiths shops, Engine house, and the dwelling house are all built of hewn timber. There is also a store house, and dwelling, smoke house &c, &c, of round logs.

September

1 FRIDAY

The weather is not as pleasant now, as it was the while we were coming up the Lakes. It is quite comfortable to sit by a fire to day. I have now got settled in my new abode and begin to feel quite at home. The grounds around the house are very neatly laid out, with graveled walks, and railings, dividing the garden into squares and beds. On these are growing thriftily, plants and vegetables, which are looking very nice, and bid fair to come to maturity, They surpass by far anything of the kind I expected to see on Isle Royale.

2 SATURDAY

It is pleasant to day, and I have been for a walk. I observed near the Engine house a small patch of Wheat which was sown for an experiment, it is now nearly ripe, and looks remarkably thrifty. I observed one bunch of twenty four stalks and heads all of which came from the same root. There is several grass platts <u>now</u> about ready to be mown, it grows large and thick, and seems well adapted to the climate.

4 MONDAY

A very windy day. the white caps rolled high on the Bay all day. By nothing am I more forcibly impressed that I am in a Northern latitude than by the forrest timber, for here instead of the stately oak, &c, that we see in southern Michigan, we have but, a stinted growth of Cedar, Balsam, Fir, and poplar with now and then a sprinkling of Birch.

5 TUESDAY

I have just returned from a walk up the Bay, and was much amused at seeing a guide board to direct the wandering traveller through this densely populated City. I observed a Caution warning all persons against traveling faster than a walk over the pavements under a penalty of $10. dollars.

6 WEDNESDAY

A beautiful morning. Made enquiries for the latest news but was told that the Telegraph was out of order below Isle Royale. Took a ramble along the shore of the Lake shearching for Agates, but was not able to find any worth saving. Had a pleasant sail on the Harbor in the evening.

7 FRIDAY

Morning rather lowery, looks like rain, clears away before noon & is quite pleasant the remainder of the day. The Isle Royale & Ohio Mining Co. are erecting another building at Ransom City, Rock Harbor, designed for a furnace house I believe, the corner stone was laid this morning by Michael.

8 FRIDAY

The air is pretty cool this morning and the wind quite fresh and chilly. At 9 A.M. bundled in cloak & hood went out in a small boat to fish. sailed down the Harbor 2 1/2 miles had one bite, but lost it, stopt at the Siscowit Mining Co's location visited the grave yard there, there are only three graves in it and one of them is a man that starved to death on this Island in the month of March A. D. 1844, his wife was the only person then remaining on this Island, and she supported herself by ensnaring Rabbits,[79] We now got into our boat and came about half way home where we crossed over to a small Island oposite, launched our boat strolled about the Island for some time at length we found berries of different varieties, Whortleberries, mulberries, wild pears, & cherries and a few red Raspberries, clambered up some very high rocks and then down to a gravelly beach, where we found some very pretty stones. In attempting to step from one point of rock to another my foot slipped and I fell into the water, this was my first <u>bath</u> in Lake Superior. Mr. Douglass helped me out and rang my clothes, and then made all possible speed for home.

9 SATURDAY

Feel the effects of my cold bath a little this morning, but not half as much so as I expected. think I shall be more cautious in future. The air seems cold enough for snow. I can hardly keep warm by the stove the wood is green pine and very wet at that.

11 MONDAY

Just returned from a fine pleasure excursion, thirteen miles up the Lake. Sailed from Ransom City at half past eight o'clock in the Morning had a good breeze for sailing most of the way and four men to row when we had not wind enough for sailing. Arrived at Mr. Mathews place[80] at 12 A.M., found them all well and taking their ease in smoking, fishing, picking berries and putting up log houses. on our way up passed Chippeway harbor, & Pigeon Bay, both very pleasant places.[81] we stopt about Two hours then started for home, having a very favorable wind, by the aid of which our little favorite the 'General Scott' took us home in good time.[82] when we got down as far as the point where we enter the harbor, we landed and feasted for nearly an hour upon berries and wild pears, then returned home, it was 5 o'clock, well pleased with our excursion and a pretty good appetite for supper, although we took a pail of luncheon with us and tents and blankets in case the wind should oppose us, so that we could not return at night. The shore of the Lake is beautiful, the rocks descend off into the water in some places, between which are numerous groves and arbors.

12 TUESDAY

A beautiful day. Mr. Shaw came up with his family and paid us a visit.[83] they are stopping about six miles below us. they came to Isle Royale from Toledo, Ohio. We think it is quite a treat to have a visit from our friends, and neighbors, away up here, and take far more pains to go to see our friends than we should in a thickly settled place.

13 WEDNESDAY

Had a severe frost last night, which bit our vines badly, it looks like fall of the year now, to see things killed down so by frost. Towards night a very high wind which prevented Mr. Shaw from reaching home, & continued to blow hard through the night.

14 THURSDAY

Commenced raining in the Morning continued until about noon when it cleared away quite warm and pleasant. Am looking for Propeller Independence daily, I might say hourly. feel very anxious to hear from home. It is four weeks to day since I left my friends in Detroit and I have not heard from them yet. There has been no boat in to Rock Harbor since we came.

15 FRIDAY

Finished the reading of the empress Josiphene's Secret Memoirs[84] last Eve—much pleased with the account M'LLE Le Normand gives of her life. think Josiphene possessed many excellent qualities of mind & heart. Were aroused twice during the night by the cry of the fowls they were pursued by a Lynx who took several of them. Mr. Douglass fired at him but missed his aim. Went out for a sail in the afternoon, the wind was in our favor when we went over, but against our returning. we finally succeeded in crossing the bay over to Mr. Hubbards location where we got another man who with Mr. Allen succeeded in rowing the boat home by dark.[85] just as we came in sight Mr. Douglass had started out in a big Mackinaw boat with all the men he could muster to come in pursuit of us.

16 SATURDAY

To day operations were commenced in the smelting furnace. I went over to see them smelt. the slag looked beautiful when running from the furnace. the ore they used to day contained very little copper, it was nearly all rock. Mr. Douglass says he had much better success than he expected to have with the first trial.

18 MONDAY

A very lowery day. Mr. McCuller[86] came over yesterday from the opposite side of the Island, and returned this morning. he came around in a boat. he says it is about 30 miles round the way he came and eleven to go on foot across. there is a trail a part of the way, & one small lake to cross. I went out in a boat just at night to see the fisherman set the net.

19 TUESDAY

It continues to be very rainy to day. I think the Equinoxal storm has commenced. The net that I went out to see set last Evening was taken up this morning full of beautiful fish. they were all very large. many of the Fish we have here are equal to the finest Salmon Trout.

20 WEDNESDAY

A very dull day. In consequence of the late rain business is at a stand at the flourishing City of Ransom. When the weather is pleasant I can hardly resist the temptation of being out in the open air, when it is stormy I am obliged to remain in doors.

21 THURSDAY

The clouds have cleared away, and the Sun is shining very pleasantly but the wind is quite chilly. Mr. Douglass has been much engaged with the smelting department, that I have seen him but once to day. It is a pleasant walk from here to the Engine house and when he is engaged there I go over some times two or three times during the day.

22 FRIDAY

A lovely morning the sun shines very warm and pleasant, although it froze ice a quarter of an inch thick last night. I dreamed I saw a vessel come into the Harbor, and I wish it would come to pass soon.

23 SATURDAY

Rather pleasant in the morning, but quite rainy in the after part of the day. Mr. M'Culluch arrived from the other side of the Isleand about noon, he came in hopes to meet the Propeller, being anxious to return home to Pittsburgh.

25 MONDAY

The Sun shines quite pleasant but the wind is very chilly, and I find a good fire very comfortable to sit by. The wind continued to blow so hard that Mr. Matthews was not able to start for home until near Evening.

26 TUESDAY

I have been very busily engaged in drawing to day. Mr. M'Culloch and his men left in the morning to go around the Island, he went with them as far as the point and then came back on foot in hopes to meet a vessel here tomorrow morning.

27 WEDNESDAY

No Propeller yet. There was a hard shower last night. it is very windy this morning. James Allen, Mr. M'Culloch, and Mr. Douglass have gone up to visit the Epidote about six miles distant.[87] they crossed the Bay in a small boat and walked through the woods. the Lake being so rough they were unable to go in a boat.

28 THURSDAY

A very rainy day and nothing to stir the dull monotony until about 3. P.M. the cry of Propeller was heard. now all was bustle and confusion, immediately the flag was hoisted and salutes fired to arouse those who should be at a distance. Mr. Giddings of Cleaveland one of the directors of the co. came up and is to remain over 'till the next trip of the boat. I had a room full of the passengers who came in to visit me while the boat stopt—most of them acquaintences. They staid nearly as long as the boat did, consequently I did not retire to bed until after midnight.

29 FRIDAY

The wind blows very hard and the Lake is very rough. Mrs. Mathews came up yesterday on the Propeller, she is staying with me, she says they had a very stormy passage, and she is congratulating herself to day that she is on 'terra firma'. I received two letters from home, and I feel much more contented this morning than I did yesterday, after hearing they were all well at home.

30 SATURDAY

A very pleasant morning, the sun shines brightly and looks red and warm as it does in July, continues very pleasant through the day. The men are all very busy building a kiln for burning char-coal. Mr. Giddings and every one about the premises have lent a helping hand. Mrs. Mathews and I walked over where they were at work, and were invited to assist, but declined doing so.

October

2 MONDAY

The Sun shines very pleasantly to day, but the wind blows quite chilly. We had some fears for the safety of some men, that were coming around the

Island in a boat. they arrived about 8 in the Evening. Mr. Giddings came in just at night and said he wished I would give him credit for half a days work in my journal of to day I promised him I would, so I have kept my word.

3 TUESDAY

It is very rainy to day. I think if stormy weather affects business matters in every place as much as it does in this <u>small city</u>, it must leave many blanks in the course of the year. Mr. McCulough started for home in a boat about noon.

4 WEDNESDAY

The weather being pleasant and the waters of the Bay so quiet that Mrs. Mathews and myself ventured out in a boat alone with a half breed woman, she managed the boat just as well as a man. We went out around the point of the Island and went ashore at a place where the Indians had camped, it is a lovely spot, & at this season the woods are beautiful. The frost has changed the foilage to bright yellow and red colors, these mingled with the unchanging green of the Cedar, Spruce, and balsom, form a beautiful contrast for the eye to rest upon.

We wandered about for some time in the woods and on the bank of the Lake, where we found some beautiful stones, Mrs. Mathews trimed my hood with moss and Kilikinic, (a weed that the Indians smoke for tobacco,)[88] we then returned home quite pleased with our trip. feeling very independent that we were able to go out alone.

5 THURSDAY

Mr. Giddings, Mr. Mathews & Mr. Douglass left us very early this morning to visit the Datholite & Epidote veins, they crossed the Bay in a boat, then walked to Epidote. being about tired out, they got some men and a boat and proceeded on to Datholite. The Lake being very rough they were unable to return home. I waited until ten o'clock for them but 'no come'.

6 FRIDAY

A very rainy unpleasant day. Our gentlemen returned home about 3 in the afternoon, wet enough, they came down in a Mackinaw boat. The air is quite warm the wind blowing from the South.

7 SATURDAY

A bright and very clear morning, and continues very pleasant through the day. Have been over to the Engine house <u>only twice to day</u>. I sometimes feel as though I was squandering away my time to be out so much, but these feelings are soon over-ballanced by the thought that a long (and I suppose very severe,) winter is close at hand, when I shall probably have to be confined in the house most of the time. But should the much dreaded winter weather be as pleasant accordingly, as it has been thus far, I shall be very agreeably disappointed. for I supposed I should be obliged to stay in the house nearly all the time.

9 MONDAY

About 8 o'clock this morning the sail vessel Algonquin[89] appeared at Rock Harbor, bringing us our winter supplies, and also the sad intelligence of the loss of the Propeller Goliath on the 14th Sept.[90] she was blowed up with gunpowder on Lake Huron off Point aux Barques, all on board was lost, it is said there were thirty passengers. Mr. Mc'Culough and two of our men went away on the Algonquin. She remained here all day, unloading freight, and one might have well said the City presented rather a busy appearance.

10 TUESDAY

It is quite still here to day. Our family is quite reduced to what it was yesterday. Mr. Mathews and family having left last evening together with those in the Algonquin, make some difference in our circle. The morning was very pleasant, but the wind became very chilly towards evening.

11 WEDNESDAY

A lovely morning, the weather is very fine and has been for several days. One would hardly expect such weather on Lake Superior at this season of the year.

12 THURSDAY

Our fine weather of yesterday has changed to day, it is very cold, with a strong North East wind. The waters seem fairly mad. I think I should rather be on terra firma than on the Lake to day. Mr. Giddings appears to feel quite uneasy now about going home.

13 FRIDAY

Rained last night, cleared away pleasant this morning, thought it bid fair to be a pleasant day. Went out for a ride in the Gen. Scott with Mr. Giddings and Mr. Douglass, soon after breakfast. We took four boatmen with us, we had a fine breeze to sail down the Bay with, but before we got to Mr. Hubbard's, we were overtaken with a shower. we stopt there a short time until it cleared away. They rowed the boat and sang in French. I don't expect many more rides this fall.

14 SATURDAY

A very pleasant day. Nothing doing of importance. one boat load of provisions shipped for Datholite. I had forgotten to say that Mr. Douglass arose very early this morning, and started before day light for Epidote. he returned about eleven A.M.

16 MONDAY

A very cold day with a very strong wind. Mr. Giddings is almost crazy for fear we shall not have a vessel in time to take him home.

17 TUESDAY

Pleasant again this morning. the Sun is quite warm to day. Nothing of importance doing in our quiet little town to day.

18 WEDNESDAY

I have been very busily engaged to day making a comforter and had just completed it when the Algonquin appeared in sight. She came direct from La Point here. On leaving here last Monday week she went across to the Ontonagon for a load of potatoes for us and in attempting to come back here, when very near the entrance of the harbor on Sunday last, the wind changed, and drove her to La Point. She brought no mail, consequently I did not receive any intelligence from home.

19 THURSDAY

The Algonquin is still here waiting for a favorable breeze to go down with, it is nothing but confusion here to day. Mr. Mathews and his family are here waiting to go down. People from all the different locations assemble here whenever a boat comes in, and some of them make it a port of holiday. I think Ransom should be classed among the Seaport towns.

20 FRIDAY

It realy seems good to be quiet this morning, after the bustle of yesterday. the boat left here about 12 last night, when Mr. Giddings, Baltie, Mathews and family took leave for Sault-Ste-Marie.

21 SATURDAY

Arose this morning quite early, and saw for the first time this fall a few flakes of snow, it very soon melted away and the day was quite warm and pleasant. Mr. Douglass went up to Datholite very early in the morning and returned about four in the afternoon.

23 MONDAY

This day would make the old adage true of "Many a bright and sun-shiny morning has turned to a dark and lowery day." The men are improving the time making preparations for winter, puting up stoves, mending broken windows, plastering up the walls, &c., &c.

24 TUESDAY

A very pleasant day but quite cool. assisted Mrs. Veale[91] to make a comfortable to day. I think we shall have snow very soon from the feeling of the air to day.

25 WEDNESDAY

Arose quite early this morning and went with Mr. Douglass in the Mackinaw up to the head of the bay, took with us four French voyaguers to row the boat, one of them being a very excentric old fellow made a deal of sport for us. The Bay is beautiful above this place, had a very pleasant ride, and returned home just in time for dinner.

26 THURSDAY

The morning was cold and cloudy, but the sky cleared about ten o'clock, the sun made its appearance, the air filled with smoke with every indication of the Indian Summer.

Mr. Douglass started for Datholite early in the morning, but was soon obliged to return on account of the wind, being so strong against the boat.

27 FRIDAY

We have to day a continuation of yesterdays pleasant weather. The Aurora borea allis were beautiful last evening. It was ten weeks yesterday since I left home, and I have been able to get only two letters and they both came at one time, and were written soon after I left. It is two months today since the date of the last, and I begin to feel quite anxious to see a boat come in. If we could have a mail say once a month I think I should be quite contented. After dinner we took a sail down to Mr. Shaws, spent the afternoon and returned home in the evening.

28 SATURDAY

The weather is delightful to day. I think I never breathed so pure air, as I have done on Isle Royale. I was much pleased with the situation of Mr. Shaws place yesterday.[92] his dwelling is situated on the border of a little bay, almost shut in by land, and forrest trees for shade, and protection from the cold and snow of winter. We have a beautiful channel of deep water, varying from 1/2 to a mile in width, extending about 15 miles in front of us, almost completely land-locked by clusters of small Islands from the Lake. This Bay or channel seldom gets very rough, so that we go out in boats with perfect safety at almost any time. We went from here down to Mr. Shaws upon it, without going out into the Lake at all. it has sufficient depth of water to float the largest steamboats.

30 MONDAY

The weather to day is somewhat changed from yesterday, being quite rainy and unpleasant. The Northern Lights were beautiful last evening, more brilliant than I have seen them before in a long time. I fear the pleasant weather we have enjoyed of late is going to change if it has not already, from all appearances of the atmosphere to day.

31 TUESDAY

A severe North East snow storm. Mr. Hubbard who has spent two winters here, remarked he thought winter was now settled upon us, others seem to think we shall have more open weather before winter sets in, time will tell.

November

1 WEDNESDAY

A continuation of yesterday's snow storm with very high winds. the thermometer standing at 29°. Four of Mr McCullough's men from the opposite side of the Island came round in a boat yesterday in expectations of finding their winter stock of provisions here which they expected on the Algonquin, but they were quite disappointed on finding no provisions nor vessel either.

2 THURSDAY

Slight flurry's of Snow continue through the greater part of the day. I think I shall not be able to go out riding in a boat after this, this fall. I would like to change the boat for sleigh and horses if I could, but, I may as well stop wishing before I commence, for if I had the sleigh and the horse, then I have not the roads. and as the ice is not considered very safe here at any time in the winter to go out upon, they would do me no good.

3 FRIDAY

The weather is quite mild and pleasant to day, and I am in hopes it will continue a while, at least, until we have a vessel from the Sault de Ste Marie. perhaps one might say this was a selfish wish. I am willing to admit this, feeling justified in it, as I have only heard from <u>home</u> but once since I left, it being already eleven weeks. it is a long time for me to be without any communications from my friends, but there will in all probability be longer periods than this before next Spring that I shall be without any knowledge of them. but for all this it appears to me as though I must hear from them again, before winter closes upon us.

4 SATURDAY

A very severe snow storm with high winds from the North East it seems to be the minds of those who have wintered at this place previous to this, that winter has fairly commenced, and that the Algonquin will not return here again this fall. To me this is a gloomy idea, however if it is to be so, I can not help it, and I will endeavor to submit without murmuring. the Snow is now fourteen inches in depth. the thermometer standing at 32°.

6 MONDAY

The morning was clear and pleasant although snow fell during the night previous, to the depth of two or three inches, making an average depth now on the ground of sixteen inches. Now, if I was in reach of home, with such sleighing as this, I think I should go there pretty quick. Mr. Veale and family are moving up to Epidote to day in a Mackinaw boat, so that now the whole population of Ransom City consists of our own household.

7 TUESDAY

I have been waiting all day to have it stop snowing before I opened my journal, but there is no more prospect of its ceasing now, than there was early this morning. I do not know but we shall all be burried up in snow, I am sure we shall, if it continues in this way much longer. I never before saw the Winter commence in any place, as it has done here at this time. The ground was not, neither had been frozen, when the snow fell. The weather had been uncomonly pleasant for some time previous to the first snow storm which commenced on the last day of October.

8 WEDNESDAY

It is quite pleasant this morning, the thermometer standing at 9° above zero. As yesterday was the day for holding elections in all the states, and as Ransom City has not as yet been incorporated and no elections made here, our men assembled in the Hall in the Evening and had a 'little jollification'. they drank to the candidates of both parties and also to Mr. Douglass and myself. I suppose in the region of the Magnetic Telegraph it is known ere this time who is President of these United States.[93] I for one think it quite doubtful whether the inhabitants of Isle Royale know who to hurrah for, before next spring. Snow fell to the depth of six inches yesterday.

9 THURSDAY

Frequent flurrys of snow continue through the day. Mr. McCullough's men left for home to day, having come to the conclusion that it was hardly worth a while to wait for a boat any longer, as the prospect at present is quite dark. Mr. Douglass let them have some provisions, so they could get along with what they had before, until Spring. They have been waiting here now for more than a week thinking the boat might possibly arrive.

10 FRIDAY

The weather is moderating to day and the snow I think is going to take its departure. I should be glad to see it go, the thought of being burried up with snow from now until the first of May is not very pleasant.

11 SATURDAY

It is thawing very fast, some rain accompanied by a South wind. My expectations are now raised in regard to the vessels coming so much, that I stand at my window a good share of the time watching to see if I can not discern her coming at a distance.

13 MONDAY

It is warm and pleasant now, the snow is melting off fast About 3 P.M., to our watchful eyes, and great joy, the long looked for Algonquin came in to our harbor, bringing us a well filled mail, and sundry other comforts for the Winter. I received two letters from home, after reading them again and again I sat down to answer them, and was so engaged that I did not retire until after midnight. I received several packages of Newspapers but shall not attempt to look at them until after I get through with the letters.

14 TUESDAY

The wind being unfavorable for the vessel to proceed on to La Point, the Capt. concluded to remain here through the day, thinking the weather might be more favorable for him tomorrow. Consequently I have spent the day in reading and answering letters. I do not know how, where, or when to stop. It does not seem as though I could seal up my letter that is to go to my home, I want to say so much. It appears to me as though it was the last opportunity I should have of sending any communication to them this winter.

15 WEDNESDAY

The Algonquin took her departure this morning about nine o'clock, for the Sault de Ste. Marie, the wind continued the same as yesterday, unfavorable for going to La Point and quite favorable for returning to the Sault. I sent a package of nineteen letters by her. She brought up a lot of dry goods, and groceries, and some more provisions. Mr. Giddings sent us a barrel of very nice cranberries, with the provisions, which we consider quite a luxury, in this country where there is so little fruit.

16 THURSDAY

If the Algonquin had remained here until this morning she might have gone on to La Point, the wind having changed during the night into the North. I have been quite busy to day looking over the news & helping Mr. Douglass mark the new goods. those of them that were purchased at the Sault de Ste. Marie were marked at very high prices, goods being in great demand at that place to supply the people on the South shore, who lost all their supplies on the ill fated Goliath

17 FRIDAY

In looking over the bills to day Mr. Douglass observed there was one box he had not seen, and went out to the store to see if it was there. I very soon saw him returning with the said box, on opening it he found it to be a box for me, from Mother and sister, filled with nick-nacks, among which were some delicious Peach & Pear sweetmeats and a lot of Quinces, Candies, &c, &c, In it was a letter of Oct. 26th (a later date than those received by mail) from sister Fanny saying that they supposed navigation was closed to Isle Royale this fall, but that on the arrival of the Detroit learned by her Clerk there was another vessel coming here, so she made all haste to put up a box of traps and ship to Isle Royale for our comfort during the long winter. I was sorry to hear by her letter of the death of Mrs. Ashly[94] although I had no reason to expect any thing else, as she was very low with the Consumption when I left Detroit.

18 SATURDAY

I have preserved my quinces to day and they are very nice. there were enough to fill a large jar full. I feel quite proud of my sweetmeats, for I did not expect to have any this winter, but I don't see but what I am pretty well supplied now.

Mr. Douglass arose at 3. o'clock this morning and started for Datholite in the Scott. he took four boatmen with him. it is now so late in the Season that I dislike to have him go, as he is obliged to go out into the open Lake where the shore is very bold and precipitous. however, there are two harbors they can make if it is too rough. Greatly to my surprise they returned home about 4. P.M. all safe, having had a fine breeze to sail down with.

20 MONDAY

It is a delightful morning a little snow on the ground in some places, the air is clear and salubrious. I have just returned from the longest walk I have taken on Isle Royale. the men have been making a road to draw out wood some distance back, it is frozen so as to be good walking now. Mr. Douglass invited me to go out upon it with him. I went and have had a very pleasant walk indeed it seems like spring.

We passed through a beautiful grove of evergreen trees consisting of Cedar, Spruce and fir, standing very thick and having tall straight bodies with cone like tops, forming so thick a mass, that the Sun is unable to penetrate the Earth through them. The beauty of this lovely spot is still enhanced by the meandering of a small brook passing nearly through its center. This grove is the only spared from the ravages of the fire within sight of our dwelling.

21 TUESDAY

Another beautiful day. it is so pleasant that when I look out I feel almost homesick. I think a great deal more about home when the weather is pleasant, than I do in a dark & cloudy, or stormy day. There were five Irishmen came down from Datholite to day they stopt at Epidote and got intoxicated, and in coming from that place here came near being drowned by up setting their boat, in a quarrel. they finally made the shore and left two of them on the rocks and then came down here to tell their story. Mr. Douglass let them remain there to get sober, and then sent a boat for them, thinking they might perish during the night.

22 WEDNESDAY

It is a dark and rainy day, but with my needle and Books I find no time to get lonely, I recollect an old adage that 'when the hands are busily employed the mind is content.' I think it very true, for I am quite sure if I was not engaged with something to take up my time I should be very miserable. The men that came down last evening, got sober so as to return home this morning.

23 THURSDAY

Another dark and gloomy day, but not gloomy to me, for I enjoy such weather as this (in my present abode) far better than I do the pleasant sunshine, for I think less about home then, We have to day received an invitation from Mr. & Mrs. Shaw to spend Thanksgiving day with them on Saturday the 25th of this month. if the weather will permit I think we shall go down. I have invited them here on Monday the 27th. as we have not received the Governor's appointment for the day, usually proclaimed in this month, we have thought fit to select a day ourselves.[95]

24 FRIDAY

It is a snowy blustering day, and I should not be at all surprised if this is the commencement of settled winter. It does not look much now, like going down to Mr. Shaws tomorrow. Mr. Hubbard brought me up a beautiful little Dog last week, it is very playful and is a good deal of company for me. I have named him Royale, and to shorten it call him Roy—being an Isle Royale dog, I thought fit to give him the name.

25 SATURDAY

We were unable to accept our invitation to partake a Thanksgiving dinner at Mr. Shaws to day, on account of the weather being so cold and blustering and the wind being North East we could not go down.

27 MONDAY

This being the day I have set apart for Thanksgiving we endeavored to keep it according to the best of our ability. We had a very good dinner, such an one, as I should not be ashamed of, in any place, and fourteen guests to partake of it. everything passed off pleasantly, and agreeably. Mr. Douglass walked up to Epidote in the morning and returned before noon, says the mine is looking very well, and that they had taken out considerable copper, ore that was very rich with copper I am very glad to hear there is beginni[n]g to be some prospect of the mines yiel[d]ing well the Company have expended so much, it seems time to meet with some returns. Just as we were removeing from the table two men arrived from Mr. McCulough's place on the opposite side of the Island. They came across on foot, and appeared much pleased to hear the Algonquin had been here, and brought them a man, (though he had been sick ever since he came here) and some provisions for the winter.

28 Tuesday

The weather being pleasant for this season of the year, Mr. Douglass thought the men could go around in a boat, and so take some provisions and the sick man too, so they borrowed Mr. Hubbard's large boat, and got loaded so as to leave after dinner. We are so situated here, as to render it necessary, to assist each other all we can. It is very different living on an Island as we do here, from what it is to live in, or near, any Town, especially as regards being independent.

29 Wednesday

The wind is very high to day but still it does not blow us any news for our quiet little burgh. I have gleaned nearly all I could find from the papers I received by the vessel. I received one package of newspapers from Mr. George Ehninger of New York City—who was among the passengers that called upon us, from the Propeller Independence at the time of her coming here, four weeks after our arrival. Mr. Ehninger is a very fine old gentleman and is an acquaintance of Uncle Olivers.[96] I think they were all mindful of us. Mr. Van Anden sent me a large package of late news, the Co. sent another from Cleaveland. the Editors sent us also, and there were several very late ones in the box I received from home. But a great share of them were filled mostly with political matters, which is not very interesting to me, notwithstanding this, they were all very acceptable.

30 Thursday

The wind is beginning to go down this afternoon, The men that left here on Tuesday can now have a chance to go around the point of the Island. they have probably remained at Mr. Shaw's place until now, the wind having been in such a direction since they left here that they would be obliged to stop. It is now very late in the Season to go out in boats into the open Lake, and is attended with much danger. As the Indians have not come over as they promised I think it very doubtful whether we get any communications via Ft Williams[97] from our friends this winter. I had much rather do without any, than to have any person's life endangered (as it would have to be,) in attempting to cross.

December

1 FRIDAY

This will pass for a pleasant day, all is quiet around me except my little favorite 'Roy' who barks occasionally at Frank the teamster who passes by frequently with loads of wood, but a glance from the dining room windows, shows there is life and business going on, in and around, the Engine house, the smoke ascends in thick clouds from its chimneys and also from a coal kiln at a little distance beyond. From the rocks on the North side of us we hear the clinking of the miners hammer, interrupted at intervals, with the loud sound of the blast, which sometimes shakes the roof of our log cabin.

2 SATURDAY

This morning I took a walk up the steep rocky ridge which rises nearly one hundred feet just back of our residence, from which, I had a fine view of the Harbor, and its rocky islands which separate it from the Lake, as well as an extended view of the Lake in the direction of <u>home Sweet home</u>, which brought up to fond memory many reminiscences of home & friends. I was particularly struck with the ragged appearance of the rocks, which lie in crumbled, weather beaten masses, one above another, presenting the appearance of having withstood the frost and storms of this Northern clime for Ages.

From the house this hill has a very sombre appearance, as the few small scattering evergreen trees, have been stripped of their dense foilage, and blackened by fires the past season.

4 MONDAY

This has been a clear, cold, day, the thermometer standing at only four above zero. We have now two or three inches of snow newly fallen some scattering drifts of the old remaining in different places. There is no appearance of ice as yet on the Bay, and the winter thus far, has been more open than I anticipated, I have been quite contented to remain in the house to day, it being most too cold to ramble about.

5 TUESDAY

The cold of yesterday has increased to day so as to sink the Thermometer down to zero. We were quite surprised this morning on arising to see the Bay frozen over, last evening there was no appearance of ice, and the fisherman set the nets as usual, and was obliged to brake the ice in order to get them up this morning.

6 WEDNESDAY

This morning there was a boat entered the Harbor but was unable to reach the wharf in consequence of the ice, which extends out more than half a mile, we saw no more of the boat, but the persons who were in it made their appearance at our door some time after, having landed their boat above the point and walked up the bay a short distance above our dwelling and crossed on the ice. They proved to be an Indian woman with three men, they had come down from Epidote to get some provisions.

7 THURSDAY

The wind blew from the North East during the night and broke up the ice leaveing it afloat in the Harbor.

The snow is falling thick, and fast, and has the appearance of being a deep fall of snow. I am in hopes the ice will move out of the Harbor before it becomes solid, otherwise it will take a long time for it to melt away in the Spring.

8 FRIDAY

The weather is now milder than it was the first of the week. it continues to snow to day, and it is already two feet deep. It appears to me now, that we are closely shut in for the winter. I endeavor to keep from thinking or even looking on the dark side of the picture. Did I allow myself to meditate on the situation in which we are now placed and all the circumstances connected there with I should be miserable enough—

9 SATURDAY

I was quite happy to see that the ice had moved out of our Harbor this morning the wind having changed to South West during the night. The

Thermometer shows the weather to be quite mild to day as it has risen to 32° above zero.

11 MONDAY

The weather continues snowy, A party of men came down from Epidote this morning and report the vein looking remarkably well. Just after dinner Mr. Shaw, & Son,[98] and Hubbard came up. Mr. Shaw says the bay is not frozen at all, (neither has been at his place,) and that they came up in a boat to within about 40 rods of Mr. Whittleseys, where he found so much ice as to render it necessary to leave their boat, and come up on foot. He seems quite encouraged in the Copper enterprise as he has recently found a very rich bed of native copper. Winter has not settled upon us so stern as yet, as to prevent our neighbors from visiting us occasionally.

12 TUESDAY

It has been very pleasant to day. Mr. Douglass walked up to Epidote this morning on snow-shoes. he crossed the Bay on the ice, and returned home about four in the evening. quite fatigued, the snow is so light and deep as to make very hard walking. he speaks very favorably of the Copper vein at Epidote.

13 WEDNESDAY

Another pleasant day. The ice is breaking up in the harbor. Mr. Douglass is quite lame to day, the effects of his walk yesterday, being his first walk on snow shoes this winter.

14 THURSDAY

It is rather cold to day. The Thermometer sank to 4° below Zero this evening. It is not very lively at Ransom now. the Season for parties has not commenced yet. there will no doubt be a great deal of bustle when the Season arrives.

15 FRIDAY

A lovely day. I little expected to see such weather as this, the middle of December on Lake Superior. I took a walk up to the new shaft they are sinking, this morning, something over half a mile distant, I had a very pleasant walk, there being a well beaten path, and the view from the cliffs is delightful.

16 SATURDAY

Mr. Douglass, myself and one man started from home at 9 o'clock this morning, and sailed in the Scott down to Mr. Shaws, we called for Mr. Hubbard and he accompanied us, we arrived at Mr. Shaws a little after ten, spent the day and returned home by the aid of a 'white ash breeze' at 8 in the evening. We found some ice in Mr. Shaws bay that had washed down there, (they said from Rock Harbor.) We had an excellent visit, and the pleasantest Sail I have ever taken on Lake Superior.

18 MONDAY

A very boisterous day, the storm commenced in the East & passed around to the South, Snow fell six inches in a short time. Mr. Douglass went to Epidote when the storm was most severe. Reports the mine not looking as well as when last he saw it.

19 TUESDAY

It is very pleasant over head to day, but the air seems very cold, it has been the coldest through the day, of any previous this winter. I was very much amused last Evening at perusing the following lines which I found penciled upon the blank leaf of a book under date of March 2ᵈ, 1847, Isle Royale.

> 'Here on this lonesome spot, (confound the place,)
> I wish I ne'r had seen its dismal face;
> When Winter comes, the frighten'd Sun retires,
> We sit in rags, and shiver round the fires.
> The only breakfast for us every morn,
> Is Cold Pork, Slap Jacks, or a mess of Corn;
> The tempest howls, yet I must go to work,
> Although I'm shivering like a frozen Turk.
> At night return and after gorging slaw,
> Lie down and slumber on a nest of straw.'

20 WEDNESDAY

It is clear and pleasant but still colder than yesterday. The Bay is frozen nearly out to the Passage Islands now, and only day before yesterday it was open some distance above the Engine house.

21 THURSDAY

This is decidedly the coldest day yet. The Thermometer stood at 12° below zero until 9 A.M. it then rose to 2° below where it remained during the day.

Mr. Veale came down yesterday afternoon and crossed on the new ice, he attempted to return in the evening, thinking to try the strength of the old ice, he broke through, and was so wet and frightened as to return here and wait until morning.

22 FRIDAY

This is a beautiful day. The weather has moderated considerable since yesterday. The thermometer has risen to 14° above Zero. Mr. Douglass went to Epidote this afternoon, intending to proceed from thence to Datholite in a boat tomorrow morning.

23 SATURDAY

It was eleven o'clock before I retired to rest last night. I said some time before night that I would finish the piece of work I was engaged with before I slept, consequently I had to sit up later than usual. Mr. Douglass returned home a little after six this evening, having walked from Epidote to Datholite and from thence home to day on snow-shoes. he was so fatigued as to be hardly able to stand up, when he came in, and so completely drenched with perspiration, one might have thought he had been in the water. Such over exertion must certainly be very injurious to ones health.

25 MONDAY

Christmas has come, with pleasant winter weather, and snow sufficient for good sleighing. but unfortunately for us, we have neither roads nor teams. The contrast in the manner of our spending the day is quite different from last Christmas Day, then among our friends at Ann Arbor, now, on a remote and lonely island, but I forbear to repine. we are happy here, even in this solitude, but s[h]ould be still happier if we could communicate with our friends. We have as many of the comforts of life here, as we should enjoy in almost any place. many more than one would suppose that had had no experience in this new country. We have as yet a plenty of fresh meats, such as, Beef, Fish, Fowls, Rabbits, &c. &c, together with as good vegetables as one would wish to find in any place, also a sufficiency of nick-nacks. in short everything for our health and comfort.

26 TUESDAY

The morning was rather snowy, but cleared away about noon and remained pleasant during the rest of the day. The day passed off in the usual routine of sewing, reading, writing, eating &c, &c, We brought with us a choice library, with which to employ our leisure moments, and it is a source of amusement and profit to us. We are now reading the Life and Voyages of Columbus, written by Washington Irving, which is very interesting.[99] It seems strange to us of the present day that a civilized people should have thrown so many obstacles in the way of this great discoverer.

27 WEDNESDAY

A delightful morning. Mr. Douglass proposed a walk on the ice. I gladly accepted the invitation, as I have not been out at all, for a number of days on account of the snows drifting in the walks. we walked up the Bay for some distance on the ice, and might have crossed if we had chosen, but I was cold enough to return without going fa[r]ther. I am too fond of exercise in the open air, to stay in the house long, when I can go out.

28 THURSDAY

The morning being pleasant we went out for a walk, first to the mine where the men are at work, from thence to the woods where the choppers where at work, these being the only well beaten tracks. The mine is about a quarter of a mile North of the house, and is elevated over a hundred feet above the Bay. the miners were sinking a shaft in the solid rock, which had I seen among the farming community I should have supposed they were digging a well, although it was not perpendicular towards the bottom, but slanting according to the course of the vein.

29 FRIDAY

I perceive that I am now on the last leaf of my journal which tells but too plainly that the year is fast drawing to a close, I can't help but look back and reflect upon the changes it has wrought. One year ago I was home with my friends in Detroit, on the 10th of January we left for Wisconsin passing through the Southern portion of Michigan, and the Northern part of Indiana & Illinois, stopping with new relatives at Walworth Wisconsin. after remaining with them about three months, we returned to Detroit by way of the Lakes, here we remained until August the 17th when we set sail for Isle Royale Lake Superior, where we are now obliged to remain stationed until the opening of navigation.

30 SATURDAY

Four months have now elapsed since our arrival on this Island, which one might have supposed would have seemed long, but on the contrary they have glided away almost imperceptibly. and now as the year draws to a close, we have to look back and reflect upon the fleetness of time, with its many changes, and that every rolling year adds another to our age, and draws us nigher to Eternity. and we might well say with the Poet,

'Time by moments steals away
First the hour and then the day!
Small the daily loss appears,
But it soon amounts to years:
Thus another year is flown,
And is now no more our own:
Forty-Eight! Old year! So thou
Hast for aye departed now.'[100]

Notes

1. I have been unable to locate the source of this poem, although it is similar in prosody and sentiment to poems celebrating the New Year in *The Detroit Advertiser* by Edward McGraw. Friend Palmer recalled a passage from "the poet McGraw" which began: "Hist! 'tis the ever fleeting tread of Time, /Another year is in the tomb of years." According to Palmer, this was "pronounced by Eben N. Willcox and others at the time as equal to anything Byron wrote" (*Early Days in Detroit*, 783). Ruth evidently did not remember the poem and may have had to look it up; in line 4 the word "birth" and in line 5 the word "knell" are markedly different in appearance, clearly written after the rest of the poem and slanting in the opposite direction from her usual script although apparently added by the same writer. The word "hear" in line 5 was originally left out and inserted with an "x" serving the purpose of the modern caret.

2. C. C. Douglass was patented 62.06 acres in Macomb Township, Michigan, on August 21, 1837; the location was about two miles west-northwest of Mt. Clemens, the west half of the southwest quarter of Section 31. Columbus also may have gone to Mt. Clemens to visit his sister and her husband. In 1827 C. C. Douglass's parents, Christopher and Phoebe Douglass, had established the family in Clinton Township, Macomb County, near Mt. Clemens and then ten years later migrated further west to Wisconsin. Their daughter Aurilla (or Orilla or Aurelia) Ann married Hiram Atwood on July 7, 1833, and remained in Macomb County. Hiram was born in Vermont on June 9, 1801, and "settled on Section 1, Clinton Township, in 1822, at a time when bear, deer, and wolf would come leisurely to the dooryard." A widower with four children, "he married Miss Aurilla A. Douglass, July 7, 1833, to whom were born three boys and a girl." The daughter was Phoebe A., the sons William, Hiram Douglass, and Richard. *History of Macomb County, Michigan* (Chicago: M. A. Lesson, 1882), 570, 571; Robert F.

Eldridge, *Past and Present of Macomb County* (Chicago: Clarke Publishing, 1905), 345.

3. C. C. Douglass's cousin, Samuel Townsend Douglass, eldest son of his uncle, Benjamin Douglass, probably lived on Grand River in Detroit at the time. He was engaged to Elizabeth Campbell in 1846 but they were not married until ten years later. Eventually his law career was very successful and he established a home in Grosse Isle. Born in Rutland County, Vermont, on February 28, 1814, he grew up in Fredonia, New York, and came to Detroit in 1837 as an attorney. He was a judge of the Wayne Circuit Court from 1851 to 1857. He died on March 5, 1898. (*Michigan Biographies* [Lansing: Michigan Historical Commission, 1924], 1:249–50.) Douglass was a witness, with Ruth's uncle Henry, at the wedding of Ruth and Columbus.

4. C. C. Douglass's parents lived in Walworth, Walworth County, Wisconsin. The county "was fully organized January 17, 1838. The county seat is at Elkhorn, the centre of the county. . . . The principal villages are Geneva, Delevan, Whitewater, Elkhorn and East Troy." From a population of 1,019 in 1838, the county grew to 15,039 in 1847 and 17,866 in 1850. John Warren Hunt, *The Wisconsin Gazetteer* (Madison: B. Brown, 1853), 221–22.

5. The Michigan Central Railroad was completed as far as Kalamazoo when the Douglasses traveled. Later that year it was finished to Paw Paw and reached Lake Michigan in 1849. Because of the season, the Douglasses needed to take the stage from Kalamazoo to Chicago and on to Walworth rather than try to sail across Lake Michigan from St. Joseph or New Buffalo.

6. One anonymous traveler between Three Rivers and Niles in the summer of 1848 recorded crossing Beardsley's Prairie northwest of Niles, noting that "it is rolling and one of the prettiest I have seen, the crops on it are very fine, but the road across it horrible, mud to the hubs." *Journal of a Trip to Michigan, 1848,* 9. A dozen years earlier Harriet Martineau had called Niles "a thriving town": "Three years ago, it consisted of three houses. We could not learn the present number of inhabitants; probably because the number is never the same two days together" (*Society in America,* 1:326).

7. Michigan City seemed to Harriet Martineau a model of a town in transition from frontier outpost to settled community—"Such a city as this was surely never before seen"—and noted that although it had begun only three years earlier it already had 1,500 inhabitants.

> It is cut out of the forest, and curiously interspersed with little swamps, which we no doubt saw in their worst condition after the heavy rains. New, good houses, some only half-finished, stood in the midst of the thick wood. A large area was half cleared. The finished stores were scattered about; and the streets were littered with stumps. The situation is beautiful. The undulations of the ground, within and about it, and its being closed in by lake or forest on every side, render it unique. (*Society in America,* 339)

8. A history of Lake County, Illinois, reports, "Justus Bangs and his nephew, Elihu Hubbard, came to Wauconda June 1, 1836, built a log cabin and 'kept bach' on the banks of Bangs' Lake. . . . Justus Bangs spent a long and active life in the neighborhood of which he was a pioneer." Wauconda, Illinois, is situated halfway between Chicago and Lake Geneva, Wisconsin, on a highway that traces the former stagecoach line. Charles Addison Partridge, *Lake County* (Chicago: Munsell Publishing, 1902), 630.

9. Big Foot Prairie was the prairie opening at the head of Geneva Lake (once known as Big Foot Lake, but renamed in honor of Geneva Lake in New York State); the prairie straddled the state line between Walworth, Wisconsin, and Big Foot, Illinois.

10. Ruth records a biography of her father-in-law, Christopher Douglass, in the February 22 entry. Beckwith gives a full genealogy:

> CHRISTOPHER DOUGLASS was twice descended from William and Ann, who came to Boston in 1640, and to New London about 1651. He was the son of Capt. Daniel^5 (Robert^4, Thomas^3, Robert^2, William^1) and Lydia^5 (William^4, Richard^3, William^{2,1}); that is, these were third-cousins. Christopher was born February 22, 1787, at New London, Connecticut; married Phoebe Douglass, his mother's brother William Jr.'s granddaughter. Her parents were Ivory Douglass and Phoebe Smith. He came from Cattaraugus county, New York, to section 28, Walworth, in 1837, with ten children. He was chairman of the board of county commissioners, 1840–2, and a supervisor in 1848. He was one of the earliest school commissioners. He died February 16, 1867. (Beckwith, *History of Walworth County, Wisconsin*, 1:511).

Elsewhere it is recorded that Christopher Douglass "was engaged in the extensive breaking, in 1837, on Big Foot Prairie. He entered the farm now owned by Mr. Merwin on Sec. 28. This farm he afterward sold to Mr. Williams, and settled on the Joseph Crumb farm. This farm he purchased at the land sale. He removed to the present village of Walworth in 1842, where he kept hotel for several years. He settled at the head of the lake in 1857, where he died in 1866 [*sic*]." *History of Walworth County, Wisconsin* (Chicago: Western Historical Company, 1882), 800.

Carlos Lavalette Douglass was born in Erie County, New York State, November 9, 1827, the ninth of the family's ten children and the fourth son. "C. L. Douglass was reared amid the wild scenes of the frontier. It was during his infancy that the family went to Michigan, and he was a child of only ten years when they came to Walworth. He early became inured to the arduous task of developing wild land, breaking prairie, and planting and harvesting crops. . . . In 1846 Mr. Douglass went to the copper mines of Lake Superior, where he spent about eighteen months. He then returned to the old home, and took charge of the business, caring for his parents until they were called to the home beyond" (*Portrait*, 257). Lavalette married Margaret

Stewart, daughter of Arthur Stewart, "an early settler of Rock Co." on August 29, 1849, and they had four children: Carlos S., who took over the Big Foot Mills built by Lavalette in Fontana in 1857; Horace G. and Louis C., who ran a milling business in Lake Geneva; and Ruth W. (*History of Walworth County, Wisconsin*, 800; *Portrait*, 258). The *Portrait* approvingly notes that he was elected to the state legislature in 1872 and "owns a beautiful home on Geneva Lake, together with considerable land, and has given to each of his children some real estate" (258).

Maria Louisa Josephine Douglass was the youngest daughter and tenth and final child of Christopher and Phoebe Douglass. A note in the genealogical materials in the Silas H. Douglass papers at the Bentley Library identifies her as having married someone named Hawley, who died, and then having married again: "Josephine is the one who sent her 'best respects to' her husband by Silas when Dr. Wooster said she had the cholera and would die." In fact she did not die at that time. Silas H. Douglass, in a June 19, 1854, letter to his wife Helen, wrote: "Mr. [Ransom] Shelden reports cholera at Detroit and the Sault. He left Josephine at the Sault sick with it," but in a July 2, 1854, letter to Helen, reports, "Josephine returned last night. There are two other sisters of Columbus here, Mrs. [Theresa] Shelden and Mrs. [Aurilla] Atwood, but they are so different from all my other relatives in their thoughts, habits, mode of living, &c., that I cannot go into their houses with much pleasure." A professor at the University of Michigan, Silas Douglass was touring the Upper Peninsula working on a geological survey and writing from Portage Lake at the base of the Keweenaw Peninsula. Douglass Papers, Bentley Historical Library, University of Michigan, Ann Arbor.

11. The children of Christopher and Phoebe Douglass were, in order, Oscar Houghton (born 1810), Columbus Christopher (1812), Aurilla Ann (1814), Roxanna Columbia (1816), Maria Theresa (1818), Gilbert Lafayette (1820), Phebe Lydia Angeline (c. 1825–1853), Agnes Noailles, Carlos Lavallete (1827–1898), and Maria Louisa Josephine (Beckwith, 1:511). Most of the children seem to have moved west from Michigan with their parents, although C. C. Douglass spent most of the period following that move in Michigan. In her journal Ruth refers to Roxanna, Lydia, Lavalette, and Josephine by name, and alludes to Oscar; Maria Theresa had married Ransom Shelden of Wisconsin in 1839 and they had settled in the Upper Peninsula by this time.

12. "An older brother [of Carlos Lavalette], Oscar H. Douglas, residing on Sec. 15, came to the town of Walworth the same year [1837]. He was born in Orange Co., Vt., in 1810. Married Sarah D. Goff. They have one son— Oscar W." At the time of the diary he was living in Illinois; by 1882 he had a farm near that of Carlos Lavalette. *History of Walworth County, Wisconsin*, 800.

13. In the *Wisconsin Gazetteer*, Hunt says of Walworth County in part that "through its whole extant there are small bodies of level prairie or meadow

land, and abrupt and irregular hills or knobs. A chain of these enters the county, about the middle of the northern line, and runs through the north-western corner. The greater portion of the county consists of oak openings. There are some 12 or more prairies of limited size, exclusive of low lands and marshes. There are also a few small bodies of heavy timber" (221–22).

14. On State Line Road southeast of Walworth, between Ridge and Aldrich Roads, the land rises above the plain and affords a panoramic view of Big Foot Prairie and extensive flatlands in Wisconsin and Illinois. This may be the location of Quality Hill.

15. *The Wisconsin Gazetteer* identifies Geneva Lake as being "in the southern part of Walworth County, 8 miles long, with a mean breadth of 1 mile. It is supplied mostly from springs, and discharges its waters into the Pishtaka river, through Geneva creek" (94). Other sources make it nine miles long and ranging from one to three miles in breadth. The town of Geneva was located "5 miles southeast from Elkhorn. The population in 1850 was 1533. It has 8 school districts" (94).

16. Harriet Martineau, traveling from Mount Joliet, Illinois, to Chicago in 1836, reported, "We saw a prairie wolf, very like a yellow dog, trotting across our path, this afternoon" (*Society in America*, 1:362). "Prairie wolf" was a term for coyote in the Midwest well into the twentieth century, and the track Ruth reports may have been that of a coyote. However, a popular pastime in the Midwest, to the point of extermination, was the driving and shooting of wolves.

17. Black Hawk (1767–1838), or Makataimeshekiakiak, was born near the Rock River in northwestern Illinois, at the primary tribal village of Saukenuk. In 1804, under pressure from American settlement that followed the Louisiana Purchase, Sauk leaders signed a treaty ceding all tribal lands east of the Mississippi, a decision Black Hawk opposed. During the War of 1812 he led Sauk warriors on British campaigns in Michigan, Indiana, and Ohio, and even after the war's conclusion and the election of the moderate Keokuk as Sauk war leader, he attacked American shipping on the Mississippi and defeated an American military force led by Zachary Taylor. In 1832 Black Hawk led a group of Sauks, Mesquakies, and other tribes into Illinois in an effort to establish a new village and restore the farming community they had once had in the region, but under President Andrew Jackson's orders, federal troops pursued Black Hawk's group up the Rock River Valley into southern Wisconsin and defeated them at the Bad Axe River. Black Hawk was imprisoned in Virginia for awhile and then allowed to return to his tribe, where he died in 1838. (Roger L. Nichols, "Black Hawk [Makataimeshekiakiak]," in *Encyclopedia of North American Indians,* ed. Frederick E. Hoxie [Boston: Houghton Mifflin, 1996], 76–78.) See Ruth's remarks on February 22 on the settling of Wisconsin.

18. The Fox River "rises in the north part of Waukesha county, and running south through the counties of Waukesha, Racine, and Kenosha, into the

State of Illinois, discharges its waters into the Illinois river at Ottawa, Lasalle county" (Hunt, *Wisconsin Gazetteer*, 93); the Rock River "rises in Fond du Lac county, and runs south through Dodge, Jefferson, and Rock counties into Illinois" (194).

19. Lyda or Lydia is probably Phebe Lydia Angeline Douglass, who married Newell Crooks in Wisconsin on October 25, 1840, and according to family lore eventually moved to California. Their marriage and the marriage of Agnes Noailles Douglass to Sylvester Hawver on March 27, 1842, are two marriages identifed by Beckwith (1:439) as having occurred early in the history of Walworth County, Wisconsin. A family monument in the Brick Church Cemetery near Walworth gives Phebe Angeline Crooks's date of death as May 12, 1853, at the age of twenty-seven years, four months, and two days.

20. Sister is Fanny Edgerton, Ruth's only sister. She outlived all the other members of her family and erected the Edgerton monument in Elmwood Cemetery, Detroit. She apparently never married. The monument gives her date of birth as December 18, 1819, and her date of death as July 8, 1894.

21. *The Wisconsin Gazetteer* identifies Jefferson Prairie as "a large prairie in Clinton, Rock county" (114).

22. A number of illnesses transmitted by ticks and body lice were grouped as spotted fever, including typhus, the symptoms of which included high fever, delirium, headaches, and a red rash.

23. The 1850 Wisconsin census for the town of Walworth lists Cornelius Huff, 36, a farmer, his wife Amanda, 31, and William C., 13, all born in New York State.

24. Roxanna Columbia Douglass married a Dr. Albert Worcester, whose name was usually spelled and pronounced "Wooster" by those who referred to him; he is probably the "Doctor" referred to here. A note in genealogical material in the Bentley Library from an aunt of Catherine Hulbert, one of Silas H. Douglass's daughters, claimed, "She was the brightest of them all." The family memorial at Brick Church Cemetery, Walworth, gives her date of death as October 12, 1862, at the age of forty-six. They lived in Walworth on the farm of Parker Worcester, probably Albert's father. Calla was Roxanna's daughter, Caroline, who died a few days later. In the same year, 1848, they had another daughter, Ellen.

25. I have been unable to identify Esther, who was possibly a servant in the Douglass household.

26. On March 2, 1848, Bela C. Hubbard, then thirty years old, and Sarah E. Baughman, also thirty, daughter of Rev. J. A. Baughman of Detroit, were married in a ceremony performed by Rev. James V. Watson and witnessed by John C. Baughman and Edward C. Walker. *Marriage Records from Archives of Wayne County, Michigan* (Lansing: Michigan State Library/Daughters of the American Revolution Louisa St. Clair Chapter, 1936), 5:149; *Vital Records from the Detroit Free Press* ([Detroit]: Michigan State Library/Daughters of the American Revolution, 1939), 24; *Detroit Free Press*, March 6, 1948, 2.

Hubbard's own journal is sketchy about that month; his only reference is a single sentence: "The most important event of the Mo. to me was my marriage on the 2nd inst" (Journal of Bela C. Hubbard, March 2, 1848, Hubbard Papers, Bentley Historical Library, University of Michigan, Ann Arbor). A prominent figure in Detroit commerce and society, Hubbard had been C. C. Douglass's colleague in the surveys led by Douglass Houghton recorded in Hubbard's "Michigan Geological Expedition in 1837" and his *Lake Superior Journal*. His sketch of C. C. on the 1840 expedition is the only visual representation we have of him.

27. I have been unable to locate the source of this allusion, but it is similar in sentiment and language to a poem by Samuel Woodworth, which Ruth might have known and misquoted. In "On the Death of a Child," Woodworth writes of the "spoiler stalk[ing] abroad":

> With merciless hand he crops the flower,
> And all its promised beauty flies—
> It falls beneath his baneful power,
> Its sweets are scattered in a hour;
> It shrinks, it withers, droops, and dies.
>
> *The Poetical Works of Samuel Woodworth*
> (New York: Charles Scribner, 1861), 1:226

The quote may also be Ruth Douglass's own creation.

28. William Bell was born in Berne, Albany County, New York, in 1806. According to the *History of Walworth County*, "He received a good common-school education, and in his early years of manhood was several years a teacher. In 1828, he moved to Albany, where he learned the carpenter's trade, at which he worked for eight years. In 1829, he married Miss Sarah Mosier [of Rensselaerville, NY, born 1810], and in 1837, they moved to the then Territory of Wisconsin, making their home in Walworth Co" (798). He was Walworth's first justice of the peace, postmaster, and county assessor, and in 1847, had been a member of the state constitution convention. He died in Kansas in 1876. Bell's Corners and Douglass Corners were two local trading points and a post office was established at Bell's Corners in 1839 with William Bell serving as its postmaster until 1853. The post office was later transferred to Douglass Corners, "which had been named Walworth" (440).

29. According to Hunt's *Wisconsin Gazetteer*, "Southport, Town, in county of Kenosha, being fractional towns 1 and 2 N., in range 23 E., on Lake Michigan. Population in 1850 was 363. It has 7 school districts" (209). It was later renamed Kenosha.

30. The first steamboat on Lake Erie, the *Walk-in-the-Water*, arrived in Detroit on its first trip on August 22, 1818. It made its first trip to Mackinac in 1819. "The round trip from Buffalo to Mackinac took on the average twelve days"

(Parkins, *The Historical Geography of Detroit*, 216, 218–19). Prior to the opening of the Erie Canal there were only eleven steamers in operation, but by 1840 there were seventy-two. Traffic continued to expand in the 1840s and 1850s.

Constant shipbuilding improved the design, fuel consumption, speed, and efficiency of the steam vessels on the Great Lakes. One significant advance was the screw propeller, first used on the *Vandalia* in 1842, as a substitute for the less-effective paddle wheel. "The use of the propeller allowed the placing of the engine in the rear part of the boat, making it possible to have one large hold for the cargo. This greatly facilitated loading and unloading the cargo. The reduction of the size of the engine gave great carrying capacity, and other improvements have increased the efficiency of the engines and the speed of the vessels" (220).

31.   The *Manhattan* was a wooden propeller, 330 tons, launched in 1847 in Cleveland. It maintained its Chicago-Detroit run for several years and then in 1850 was portaged into Lake Superior at Sault Ste. Marie. (Julius F. Wolf, Jr., *Julius F. Wolf, Jr.'s Lake Superior Shipwrecks*, 2nd ed. [Duluth: Lake Superior Port Cities, 1990], 4). In 1851, in shallow water off Whitefish Bay, it was sunk in a collision with the sidewheeler Monticello and recovered. (Frederick Stonehouse, *Great Wrecks of the Great Lakes* [Marquette, Mich.: Harboridge Press, 1973], 8, 42.) In 1859 it struck a bar off Grand Marais and broke up (Wolf, 8). The *Princeton* was a twin-screw propeller, 455 tons, built in 1845 by Samuel Hubbell, of Perrysburgh, Ohio. It was the first large steamer on the Great Lakes to have twin screws and was the first propeller with a cabin on the upper deck. On November 1, 1848, the *Princeton* "fouled the brig *Empire* on Lake Huron, about 45 miles off the St. Clair River" and the brig sank. The *Princeton* was eventually caught and crushed in the ice at Gravelly Bay, Lake Erie. (Erik Heyl, *Early American Steamers* [Buffalo: N.p., 1953–1969], 2:209.)

32.   The *Milwaukee Sentinel and Gazette* for Wednesday, April 19, 1848, published the following account, titled "Great Gale and Snow Storm":

> We have had since midnight on Monday, one of the severest gales ever known on Lake Michigan. The weather, which had been very fine since the first of the month, underwent a change on Monday; the clouds gathering toward evening, and the rain falling fast, accompanied with a light south-westerly wind, through the early part of the night. About 2 A.M. of Tuesday the wind suddenly shifted to the northeast and immediately commenced blowing with great violence, the rain at the same time changing to snow which began to fall, fast and furiously.— As the dawn appro[a]ched the wind seemed to increase in force, until, at 4 o'clock and, from that hour till nearly noon, it blew almost a hurricane, driving the snow before it in blinding flurries, and piling it up, along the fences and on the lee side of the streets and houses, two or three feet deep. A tremendous sea was rolling outside, and the breakers came tumbling in towards the shore with a force and

frequency betokening the violence of the elemental war. About mid-day the clouds broke, the tempest began to lull, and the sun shone again; but the wind, tho' gradually easing off, blew stiffly till night fall.

Great damage is apprehended to the shipping on the Lake from this sudden and fierce storm. A large number of sail vessels are known to be between this point and the straits. The steamers *Sultana* and *Superior* are also supposed to have passed Mackinac some time Monday night. And the propellers *Cleveland* and *Manhattan* left this port, for Buffalo, only an hour or two before the tempest came up. It is in regard to these two, especially, that a good deal of alarm is felt. They were both deeply laden and had many passengers. During yesterday a number of articles were picked up along the beach, which must have come from these propellers. Among them are two gang-way planks, a gang-way door, known to belong to the *Cleveland*, several boxes and barrels, which were shipped by her on Monday evening, and fragments of trunks. One large black leather-covered trunk, filled with woman's apparel and containing a valise full of papers, was picked up near the North Point. The letters in it are addressed to John T, Thompson, Troy, N.Y., and Coleraine, Mass., and to Louisa A. Thompson. Other documents in the valise indicated the present residence of the owners to be Rosendale, Fond du Lac County. All these may have been washed overboard by the sea, without endangering the safety of the vessel, and it is the prevalent belief that, tho' sorely tried, the propellers rode out the gale in safety.

Our Harbor has suffered severely from the storm. The sea has made a clean breach inside of the North Harbor Pier, through the neck of land, separating the river from the Lake, and has, it is feared, nearly filled up the channel. The river rose two and a half feet, reaching a higher level than it has attained at any time these two years past. As we write (6 P.M. Tuesday) the sky is again cloudless, the sun as bright as ever, and nothing but the distant roar of the still angry Lake to indicate that so fierce a storm has but recently vexed its waters and perchance buried some gallant craft in its depths.

P.S. A party who went down to the South Point yesterday afternoon, returned in the evening with a number of articles picked up on the beach. Among them was the trunk of Mr. Michael Dousman who was a passenger on board the *Cleveland*, and several articles of clothing. (3)

The following day the paper was "glad to announce that our Harbor has not suffered as much as was feared, from the effects of Tuesday's gale" (April 20, 1848, 2). A sand bank had formed "where the best water used to be found" but there was still a good channel.

33.   Hunt wrote in the *Wisconsin Gazetteer* that Racine, Wisconsin,

situated on the western shore of Lake Michigan, at the mouth of Root river . . . was first settled in 1835, incorporated as a village in 1841, and received a city charter in 1848. The city is principal-

> ly built upon a plain or table land elevated some thirty or forty feet
> above the waters of the lake . . . situated 16 miles north of the state
> line, and 25 south of Milwaukee. . . . In 1840 the population was
> 337; 1844, 1,100; 1847, 3,004; 1849, 4,002 . . . Racine has one of
> the best, if not the very best harbor on the western shore of the
> lake" (183).

34. The Manitou Islands, located off the Leelanau Peninsula, in sight of the
    Sleeping Bear Dunes, were an important wooding stop near the Straits of
    Mackinac. In 1846, when Bryant stopped on North Manitou Island, his
    party "landed and strolled into the forest" where they saw "hillocks and hol-
    lows of sand, like the waves of the lake in one of its storms, . . . covered with
    an enormous growth of trees which must have stood for centuries." They
    "admired the astonishing transparency of the water on this shore, the clean
    sands without any intermixture of mud, the pebbles of almost chalky white-
    ness, and the stones in the edge of the lake, to which adhered no slime, nor
    green moss, nor aquatic weed." William Cullen Bryant, *The Letters of
    William Cullen Bryant, 1836–1849*, ed. William Cullen Bryant II and
    Thomas G. Voss (New York: Fordham University Press, 1977), 2:444.

35. Little Fort is now Waukegan, Illinois.

36. "The City Hotel, subsequently the Sherman House, was built in 1836–37 by
    Francis C. Sherman. Jacob Russel was its first proprietor, taking possession
    in December, 1837. In 1844, Mr. Sherman remodeled the house, added two
    stories, making it five stories high, and changed its name to the Sherman
    House." A. T. Andreas, *History of Chicago from the Earliest Period to the
    Present Time* (Chicago: A. T. Andreas, 1884), 1:635.

37. The *Michigan* was a steamboat built and owned by Ruth's uncle, Oliver
    Newberry. Newberry built two *Michigans*. The first, built in 1833, was the
    second steamboat built in Detroit and at the time the largest steamer on the
    lakes; it was retired when the second *Michigan* was built and commissioned
    in 1847. It is the second *Michigan* that is undoubtedly referred to here. Built
    by Oliver Newberry, it passed into the hands of Henry W. Newberry on
    Oliver's death, then was owned by Ruth's brother, Oliver N. Edgerton,
    before going through two other owners and being turned into a tow barge in
    1865. In Ruth's time the *Michigan* shared the Buffalo-Detroit-Green Bay
    run with the *Sultana*. See also note 55.

38. These uncles were Ruth's maternal uncles, Oliver Newberry, the "Admiral
    of the Lakes," and Walter Loomis Newberry.

39. According to the 1933 edition of the *Oxford English Dictionary,* the phrase
    "'Lions' of the place" refers to "things of note, celebrity, or curiosity (in a
    town, etc.); sights worth seeing . . . derived from taking visitors to see the
    lions . . . kept in the Tower of London" (7:323). One of this dictionary's
    examples comes from *Up the Rhine* by Thomas Hood: "The rest of the day
    was spent in seeing the Lions—and first, the Cathedral, the mere sight of

which did me good, both morally and physically" (2nd ed. [Philadelphia: Porter and Coates, 1840], 110). Fredrika Bremer writes of touring Milwaukee in 1850, "In the afternoon I was driven about to see all the lions of the place in a carriage, which a gentleman of the town had placed at my disposal" (*Homes of the New World*, 1:615).

40. Milwaukee was the largest city in Wisconsin in 1848, had been incorporated as a city only two years earlier, and was the major harbor for shipping in the state (Hunt, *Wisconsin Gazetteer*, 146–50).

41. The "great fire in Detroit" was extensive. Silas Farmer claimed,

> It burned more buildings and destroyed much more property than any previous fire. . . . It originated in De Wolf's storehouse, better known as the 'old yellow warehouse,' located on the river between Bates and Randolph Streets, and was caused by sparks from the propeller *St. Joseph*, then lying at the dock. The fire extended from this point northeast nearly to the southwest corner of Jefferson Avenue and Beaubien Street, burning most of the buildings, nearly three hundred in all, south of Jefferson Avenue to the river; and from the middle of of the block between Bates and Randolph Streets to the middle of the block between Brush and Beaubien Streets,—a space equal to six squares. For many years the locality was designated as the 'burnt district.' Of the buildings burned, one hundred and seven were dwellinghouses, and between three hundred and four hundred families were left homeless. Among the more prominent buildings burned were the old Council House, the Berthelet Market, Wales Hotel or the American House, and Woodworth's Steamboat Hotel. The fire broke out at 10.30 A.M. and lasted till 4 P.M. The sparks were so numerous and so large that, east of Woodward Avenue, nearly every house had to be watched, and sparks brushed from the roofs. The whole city was alarmed, and there was great fear that the fire could not be subdued. Several buildings were blown up and others torn down, to hinder the progress of the flames. Furniture was carried for safety to points a mile distant, and many families, nearly that distance away, commenced to pack their most valuable goods. The total loss exceeded $200,000, on which there was but $34,000 insurance. Sufferers by the fire were relieved by committees of citizens.
>
> *The History of Detroit and Michigan, or The Metropolis Illustrated: A Chronological Cyclopaedia of the Past and Present* (Detroit: Silas Farmer and Co., 1884), 493.

Other sources that describe the fire include the *Detroit Free Press*, which headlined its front-page story on May 10, 1848, "Great Conflagration!" and Catlin's *Brief History of Detroit in the Golden Days of '49* (41). Friend Palmer claimed to be an eyewitness when the fire broke out in the warehouse used for "the storage, repacking and cleaning of furs, ridding them of the fatty portion adhering to them." He and Captain J. A. Whittall, United States quartermaster, saw a propeller

> just steaming away from the dock of the yellow warehouse, when suddenly an immense billowy cloud of inky smoke streaked with jets of flame burst from the rear of the building, and in less than a minute the whole structure was a roaring mass of fire. . . . The cleaning benches and floors were so saturated with the grease and oil from the furs that they were as tinder. The flames, fanned by a fierce east wind, raged despite the efforts of almost the entire population of the city until quite along in the afternoon" (*Early Days in Detroit,* 344–45)

Palmer gives a specific list of buildings that were destroyed.

42. In the August 2, 1848, edition of the *Detroit Free Press* an item appeared announcing the dissolution of the North American Mining Company and the re-organization of its shareholders into the North American Mining Company of Detroit. The action had taken place in a meeting on June 26 and C. C. Douglass was one of the signatories. His work in the Upper Peninsula may have been related to the North American holdings, although he seems to have worked for several companies simultaneously in various capacities.

43. Aurilla Douglass Atwood was C. C.'s sister. See note 2.

44. Martha T. Porter, 25, of Ann Arbor, married James C. Allen, 32, also of Ann Arbor, on May 9, 1848. *Marriages 1827–1857 in Washtenaw County, Michigan* (Lansing: Michigan State Library, 1961), 10.

45. Fanny was undoubtedly Ruth's sister, Fanny Edgerton, but I am unable to identify Ann. "Ann" may have been Ruth's cousin Mary Ann Newberry Starkweather, daughter of Elihu Newberry and married to John Starkweather of Ypsilanti, Michigan.

46. Ruth's aunt, Ruth Newberry, had married Josiah Hartwell of Sangerfield, New York in 1842. He is probably "Uncle H."

47. The *Detroit Free Press* for June 12, 1848, notes: "Died. Draper, Simeon B., in this city, on the 7th inst., of congestive fever, aged 21 years, son of Mrs. Harriet Draper, of Rochester, NY." Mrs. Felker's was probably a house where Simeon Draper boarded.

48. Henry White may have been a blacksmith, later a boilermaker, or may have been related to John Whyte, who ran a grocery in Detroit. Mrs. Shepherd may also have been a grocer. James H. Wellings, *Directory of the City of Detroit and Register of Michigan for the Year 1845* (Detroit: Harsha and Willcox, 1845); *Daily Advertiser Directory for the City of Detroit for the Year 1850* (Detroit: Duncklee, Wales, and Co., 1850).

49. Mother is Louisa Edgerton; Aunt Ruth is Ruth Newberry Hartwell; Fanny is Ruth Douglass's sister; and Oliver in this instance is probably Oliver Edgerton, her brother.

50. "The Nile was built at [Oliver] Newberry's own yard and was launched July 4, 1843," then was "rebuilt and altered in 1845. In 1846 and for a few trips

in 1847 she ran between Detroit and Buffalo, and then was shifted to the Buffalo-Detroit-Chicago route" (Heyl, *Early American Steamers*, 2:165). It survived a collision with the *Wisconsin* on August 30, 1847, and in 1848 was given additional alterations. In October 1849, it was driven aground at Milwaukee, stripped and floated, but grounded near the mouth of the Milwaukee River, where it stayed until it was destroyed by fire in September 1850.

51. Benjamin Douglass was Christopher Douglass's brother, older by two years, and C. C. Douglass's uncle. Born March 14, 1785 in New London, Connecticut, he moved with his family to Wallingford, Vermont, in 1797, then came west to Springville, New York, with Christopher in 1811. While Christopher settled in New York State for a time, Benjamin returned to Vermont, married Lucy Townsend on May 12, 1812, and then emigrated to Fredonia, New York in 1814, staying in western New York, where he served as sheriff of Chautauqua County and served in the state legislature, until 1840, when he settled on a farm near Ann Arbor, Michigan. He was the father of Samuel T. Douglass, Silas H. Douglass, and Lydia Douglass (the third of that name in the family tree, named after Benjamin's mother; Benjamin and Christopher also had a sister Lydia, who was the mother of Douglass and Jacob Houghton, Jr.). (See Douglas, *Douglas Genealogy*.) Benjamin Douglass died in Detroit, on June 16, 1848, at the age of sixty-three; the funeral was at his residence on Jefferson Avenue and the burial at Elmwood Cemetery. (See Ruth Douglass's entry for June 17, 1848.)

52. An ad for the *Detroit* for its 1846 season touted it as sailing "between Detroit and the Silver and Copper Mines of Lake Superior!!!" and described it as "entirely new, 350 tons burthen, is furnished with a new and superior engine, draws but little water, and well adapted to the Saut trade" (Wellings, *Directory . . . for the Year 1846,* 163). In 1848 its announcement in the *Detroit Free Press* ran as follows:

> The Steam Boat DETROIT Capt. J. C. Benjamin, will run during the season of 1848 between Cleveland and Sault Ste. Marie in the following manner, touching on Mackinaw each way.
>
> Leave Cleveland every Monday evening at 7 o'clock
>   " Detroit   "   Tuesday morning at 9   "
>   " Mackinac   "   Thursday   "   at 7   "
> Returning—Leaves Sault Ste Marie every Friday morning at 10
>   "   Mackinac   "   "   evening at 10
>   (August 11, 1948, 1)

53. The Ohio and Isle Royale Mining Co. was officially called the Isle Royale and Ohio Mining Company, but many references to it reverse the locations in the name, perhaps to distinguish it more easily from other companies like the Pittsburgh and Isle Royale Mining Company. Jacob Houghton, Jr., reporting on the mineral region of Lake Superior in 1846, lists the Isle

Royale and Ohio Company as having 12,000 shares and nine three-mile locations on Isle Royale. Its directors included a number of figures from Cleveland, Cincinnati, Columbus, and Toledo. One director, Philo Scoville, was also active on Isle Royale working a mine he had located on what is now called Scovill Point. Houghton, *Mineral Regions of Lake Superior*, 147.

54. Charles Mattoon Giddings, "a pioneer merchant and long a prominent and very popular citizen of Cleveland," came to the city in 1826 and established himself as a merchant in the firm of Giddings and Baldwin. He was subsequently a leading financial and social figure. He died in 1853, at the age of fifty-six, after financial reverses had forced him to give up an elegant stone house in the city and retire to a farm. The family name is spelled "Gidings" in some of his surviving correspondence and on the family tombstone in Erie Street Cemetery, Cleveland. Gertrude Van Rensselaer Wickham, *The Pioneer Families of Cleveland, 1796–1840* (Cleveland: Cleveland Centennial Com-mission, 1914), 1:310–11.

William Ives, who mapped the island in 1847, identifies one of the claims in the Ransom location as being held under Giddings's name. Materials in the Charles Whittlesey Papers at the Western Reserve Historical Society indicate that C. C. Douglass reported to C. M. Giddings on the progress of the Quincy Mine as late as July 1853. Their business involvement, then, continued beyond the period on Isle Royale.

55. See also note 37. On September 4, 1848, a few weeks after the Douglasses traveled on it, the Michigan was damaged in a collision on the Milwaukee River. The vessel continued in service until 1865. Heyl, *Early American Steamers*, 3:231–32.

56. The delta at the mouth of the St. Clair River, where it enters Lake St. Clair, had "no less than six principal, and numerous smaller channels" but only one, the north channel, was used for navigation into and out of the river. The navigation channel connecting the lake and the river was sometimes difficult to locate, particularly in fog, and many vessels ran aground on the flats. *Gazetteer of the State of Michigan* (Detroit: S. L. Rood, 1838), 366.

57. Algonac is located at the point where the St. Clair River empties into Lake St. Clair. One of its early pioneers, John K. Smith, sometimes referred to as "the father of Algonac," was the father of Lydia Reed Smith, C. C. Douglass's second wife.

58. Newport was originally called Ward's Landing and later renamed Marine City. Located at the convergence of the Bell River and the St. Clair, it had developed as a shipbuilding center for the Great Lakes trade.

59. Palmer was started in 1818 by D. C. McKinstry and Thomas Palmer. The city was located at the convergence of the Pine River with the St. Clair, and eventually was renamed St. Clair. George B. Catlin, *The Story of Detroit* (Detroit: Detroit News, 1923), 281.

60. The city of Port Huron was built at the conjunction of the Black River and the St. Clair River.

61. Located just north of the city of Port Huron, near the entrance to the St. Clair River from Lake Huron, Fort Gratiot was first established in 1814 and rebuilt in 1828. In 1847, during the Mexican War, its troops were withdrawn and it may have been idle when Ruth Douglass saw it.

62. Point aux Barques is the northernmost point on Michigan's Thumb, the peninsula separating Saginaw Bay from Lake Huron.

63. On Mackinac Island Mrs. Graveraet was the wife of Henry Graveraet, an interpreter who assisted the Indian agent, and mother of Robert J. Graveraet, a significant figure in the development of the iron mining industry around Marquette, Michigan. C. C. Douglass and Bela Hubbard stayed at Graveraet's house on Mackinac Island on their way to and from the 1840 Houghton expedition (Hubbard, *Lake Superior Journal,* 99n. 84). R. J. Graveraet arrived at the Van Anden House in Sault Ste. Marie a few days before the Douglasses, and Albert Graveraet traveled with them from Mackinac Island on the *Michigan.*

64. Thunder Bay is a large bay midway between Saginaw Bay and the Straits of Mackinac, located in Alpena County. The two islands, Thunder Bay Island and Sugar Island, are in Lake Huron, just outside the bay.

65. Presque Isle is a peninsula jutting into Lake Huron and forming a harbor with another point further south. Presque Isle County takes its name from the peninsula.

66. Joshua W. Van Anden, originally from New York City, had been the manager of the American Hotel in Detroit, a building that had been remodeled from the residence of Governor Hull and was visited by such prominent figures as Harriet Martineau, Anne Jameson, Frederick Marryat, and former president Martin Van Buren. Van Anden established the Van Anden House in Sault Ste. Marie in 1845 and ran it until 1853. He advertised, "This house has been extensively enlarged, newly finished and furnished, and a portion expressly fitted up for the accommodation of Ladies and Families. The location is in full view of the Falls, with fine prospects of the river up and down" (*Lake Superior News,* August 8, 1846, 4). He moved to Ontonagon and opened the Bigelow House in July 1854, and finally established the Douglass House in Houghton in 1860. He died of stomach cancer on October 9, 1861, at the age of forty-nine (Burton Historical Collection Obituary Index). At the time of the Douglasses' passage through Sault Ste. Marie, the second hotel in town, the Algomah House, had been refurbished and renamed the Ste. Marie Hotel.

67. This group contained members of families with some status in the region. Dunning R. McNair of Kentucky was appointed assistant mineral agent by the secretary of war on July 29, 1845. McNair replaced George Saunders as assistant to John Stockton, superintendent of mineral lands, Lake Superior. The Mineral Land Agency was based in Copper Harbor, at Fort Wilkins. In

1847 Congress transferred the authority to sell mineral lands from the military to a new civilian agency. When Fort Wilkins was closed and the command transferred to Fort Brady at Sault Ste. Marie in 1846, Col. McNair entered into an agreement for "the safekeeping and accountability of the public property" at the fort (Lawrence T. Fadner, *Fort Wilkins, 1844, and the U.S. Mineral Agency, 1843, Copper Harbor, Michigan, Lake Superior* [New York: Vantage Press, 1966], 75–78). According to Don H. Clarke's *United States Mineral Agency* (N.p., 1973), "Col. D. R. McNair remained as a sub-agent for 1848 at a salary of $125.00 per month to ease the transfer of land from the War Department to the Chippewa Land District" (24).

Mrs. McKnight was the wife of Sheldon McKnight, an assistant to the superintendent of mineral lands in 1845, based in Sault Ste. Marie. In the early days of Lake Superior shipping, before the construction of the Soo Locks, McKnight hauled cargo with a horse-drawn cart across the portage at Sault Ste. Marie, and by 1850 established, in partnership with J. T. Whiting, a strap railroad between the two landings, using horse-drawn carts on the tracks. He also owned docks at Sault Ste. Marie and was involved in shipping throughout the Great Lakes.

68. John St. John described this vessel as "Independence, propeller, owned by Capt. Bristol and Co., commanded by Capt. Bristol, many years a skilful [*sic*] navigator of the lower lakes. She is 280 tons, a good sea vessel, and of the propeller speed. She has good cabins and accommodations, and will probably leave alternately with the [Julia] Palmer" (*A True Description of the Lake Superior Country* [New York: William H. Graham, 1846; reprint, Grand Rapids: Black Letter Press, 1976], 109). Lewis Marvill reported to the Pioneer Society of Michigan that he was both steward and waiter for the inaugural voyage of the *Independence* between Sault Ste. Marie and Copper Harbor in the spring of 1845, and that C. C. Douglass was one of the passengers, on his way to the Cliff Mine ("First Trip by Steam to Lake Superior," 67–69).

69. The falls and rapids of the St. Mary's River made access to Lake Superior from the river impossible. For a certain period after vessels were either hauled across the portage or shipped in parts for original assemblage on the lakeshore, vessels shipping copper and iron ore would need to unload their cargo above the falls, transport it overland, and reload it onto other vessels on the lower lakes end of the portage, a costly and time-consuming method that ended with the opening of the Soo Canal in 1855.

70. *The Bachelor of the Albany* by Marmion Wilmo Savage was a new (1848) novel, published not with the author's name but with the reassurance that it was "by the author of *The Falcon Family* and *My Uncle the Curate*." Bonamy Dobrée writes of Savage that he "had all that admirable Victorian geniality, that incurable optimism, that touching belief that all men are good if only they can see they are, which makes us at once love and suspect Dickens. . . . A lesser novelist, Savage probably represents the average atti-

tude toward life of his day far better than the greater worthies." Dobrée, introduction to *The Bachelor of the Albany [by Marmion W. Savage]* (New York: Frederic A. Stokes, 1928), 7–8.

71. Fort Brady was built on the American side of Sault Ste. Marie in 1823, and succeeded Fort Wilkins as the site of the U.S. Mineral Land Agency.

72. Horace Greeley, the well-established editor of the *New York Tribune*, was an investor in the North West Mine. He recounts his travels in the copper region in 1847 and 1848 in *Recollections of a Busy Life* (New York: J. B. Ford and Co., 1868). The *American Mining Journal and Railroad Gazette* reprinted his letters to the *New York Tribune* about both trips; an 1848 letter was dated September 1 and focused primarily on the Cliff Mine.

73. La Pointe, Wisconsin, was the site of the annual government payment to Ojibwa and Pottawatomi tribes under the terms of treaties that opened up Indian lands to settlement and development. Charles Lanman described the area as "contain[ing] about a dozen inhabited log cabins, and the wigwams of about three thousand Chippeway Indians . . . assembled there to receive their annual instalment [*sic*] in money and goods from the general government, as a return for the untold acres, which they had deeded to their 'Great Father and Protector,' the President." Each Indian received "four dollars in money, and in goods one blanket and a sufficient amount of cloth to make a pair of leggins," after some of them "had paddled their canoes more than a thousand miles" and "reached the Point in a state of starvation," which made them "immediately compelled to transfer their money into the open hands of the American Fur Company, for pork at *fifty* dollars per barrel and flour at *fifteen* dollars per hundred." Lanman was particularly derisive about the end of this meeting: "It was understood, however, that when the red barbarians should start for their distant homes, the white barbarians would furnish them with sufficient provisions to take them out of sight" (*A Summer in the Wilderness*, 134).

74. John St. John described the *Napoleon* in 1846 as "new and beautiful, well arranged, found, and rigged vessel, of 180 tons, as floats any waters in the world" (*A True Description of the Lake Superior Country*, 109). The schooner was built at St. Mary's and was owned by Ruth's uncle, Oliver Newberry.

75. Copper Harbor was the first site of the Mineral Agency, begun in 1843 and located in 1846 on Porter's Island in the harbor. Alvah L. Sawyer, *History of the Northern Peninsula of Michigan and Its Peoples* (Chicago: Lewis Publishing, 1911), 1:336.

Eagle Harbor, also occupied in 1843 by mining explorers, is located fifteen miles west of Copper Harbor. In 1846 Lanman observed:

> The two principal log cabin cities of Point Keweenaw are Copper Harbor and Eagle River. The former is quite a good harbor, and supports a vacated garrison, a newspaper, a very good boarding-house, and several intemperance establishments. The

latter has a fine beach for a harbor, a boarding-house, a sawmill, and a store, where drinking is the principal business transacted. The number of resident inhabitants in the two towns I was unable to learn, but the sum total I suppose would amount to fifty souls.

Altogether perhaps five hundred miners and clerks may be engaged on the whole Point, while about as many more, during the summer, are hanging about the general stopping places in the interior. This brotherhood is principally composed of upstart geologists, explorers, and location speculators (*Summer in the Wilderness*, 154).

Horace Greeley, writing in September 1848, thought, "Copper Harbor is even less stirring and thrifty than it was [fourteen months earlier]; Eagle Harbor not more so, and the only improvement in the interim is a cheap pier pushed into the harbor from the west, at which any vessel on the Lake may safely lie and unload in any weather" ("Lake Superior," 58). Eagle River was the location of the Lake Superior Copper Company, which obtained leases in 1843 and was later managed by C. C. Douglass in 1846.

76. Located in Lake Superior off the northern shore of Wisconsin, the Apostle Islands had long been an established base for the American Fur Company's trade with region tribes. Because so much trade and travel in the Lake Superior region necessarily took place during the summer, the annual gathering of Indian tribes for government payment has frequently been commented on by travel writers. (See note 21 above for information on La Pointe.) C. C. Douglass visited the islands first on the 1840 Douglass Houghton expedition, recounted in the published journals of both Bela Hubbard and Charles W. Penny.

77. Dr. John S. Livermore was a native of Oneida County, New York, as was Ruth Douglass, and practiced medicine in New York until he moved to Oakland County, Michigan, in 1830. "In 1848, he was appointed Indian Sub-Agent for the Chippewas of Lake Superior and the Upper Mississippi, and served as such three years, with headquarters at La Pointe." He also lived and practiced medicine in Marquette and Copper Harbor until his death in 1862 (*History of the Upper Peninsula*, 284).

78. The Ontonagon River empties into Lake Superior east of the Porcupine Mountains. Henry R. Schoolcraft's expedition of 1820 navigated the river and reported on the Ontonagon Boulder, a copper mass. Douglass Houghton explored the region with the Schoolcraft expedition of 1831, and returned in 1840. In 1844, C. C. Douglass "came to the Ontonagon to explore the locations the various [mining] companies had made under [the 1843] government permits, with the view of opening up mining operations" (*History of the Upper Peninsula*, 511). The Douglasses would return to the region after their period on Isle Royale.

79. The Siskowit Mine was across from Mott Island, named for Charlie Mott, whose death by starvation and whose wife's survival is recounted in *The*

Honorable Peter White, by Ralph Williams. C. C. Douglass was one of the people who came to the island with the Motts when they were hired to winter over on a mining site. (See note 92 in Notes to Introduction.)

80. Mr. Matthews's place was the Isle Royale and Ohio's Datholite Mine location on the south shore. Mark Matthews succeeded Leander Ransom as the agent for the Ohio and Isle Royale and was superceded by C. C. Douglass. As superintendent earlier in 1848 he had initiated the Datholite and Epidote locations on the south shore. Epidote Mine was located midway between Saginaw Point and Chippewa Harbor on the island's thumb, which extended up to the passage into Rock Harbor across from Ransom, and Datholite Mine was further west, between Chippewa Harbor and Siskowit Bay, about a dozen miles overland from Ransom. Matthews's wife became Ruth's closest companion on the island.

81. Chippewa Harbor is the protected harbor on the south shore of Isle Royale, about six miles overland from Moskey Basin, at the western end of Rock Harbor, and about ten miles overland from the present Daisy Farm Campground, where the town of Ransom was situated. Pigeon Bay may possibly be either the present-day Tonkin Bay or Conglomerate Bay, both a short distance south of Rock Harbor.

82. The company sailboat *General Scott* was named after the "Gen. Scott, 240, Huron, Ohio, 1839, sunk in Lake St. Clair by collision, in 1848." *History of St. Clair County, Michigan* (Chicago: A. T. Andreas, 1883), 436.

83. Cornelius G. Shaw worked the Smithwick site on the island, initiated by James Smithwick in 1843 and located not far from Scoville's mine. His diary of the previous summer's work on the island (1847) is one of the best sources for knowledge of the mining life of the period. Originally from western New York, he and his wife, Sallie Starr Shaw, came to Michigan in 1831, and settled in Toledo, Ohio, in 1832. "He is said to have built the first frame house in Toledo." Clark Waggoner, *History of the City of Toledo and Lucas County, Ohio* (New York: Munsell and Company, 1888), 665.

    A carpenter and joiner by trade, Shaw was deputy to the first sheriff of Lucas County, and served two terms as sheriff himself. According to Waggoner, "He was connected with a Copper Mining enterprise at Isle Royal, Lake Superior, in 1847–1848, and returned to Toledo in 1849" (665). Returning by steamer from California in 1850, he and a number of other passengers contracted cholera in Acapulco and died at sea. His widow died in Toledo in 1886. The Smithwick Mine seems to have been abandoned with his departure from the island. (See also note 40.)

84. The two volumes of *Historical and Secret Memoirs of the Empress Josephine* by M'lle M. A. Le Normand were translated by Jacob M. Howard in 1847 (Philadephia: John E. Potter, n.d.). Le Normand had earlier written several books about historical women.

85. James Hubbard was the agent of the Siskowit Mine, under Charles Whittlesey.

86. H. H. McCullough was the agent and mining superintendent for the Pittsburgh and Isle Royale Mining Company location at Todd Harbor. His name is spelled in a variety of ways by Ruth and others. The operation was begun in 1846 and was the only flourishing north shore mine during the first period of extensive work on the island. It closed in 1854, which made it one of the most long-lived, along with the Siskowit Mine. In July 1848 there were nine men at work on the site (Lane, "Part I: Isle Royale," 6). When McCullough left the island in October, he reported to the *Lake Superior News* that the shaft had been sunk twenty feet and that the crew would continue working through the winter (October 28, 1848, 2).

87. See note 80.

88. By "Kilikinic" or "Filikinic" (the handwriting is difficult here) Ruth Douglass means "kinnikinnick" (also spelled "kinnikinnic" and "killikinick"), a word derived from Algonquian, referring to a tobaccolike mixture of dried leaves and bark for smoking. She may be referring more specifically to a plant from which the leaves or bark for such a mixture are taken, called bearberry: "a low plant which creeps along the ground with small pinkish-white lantern-shaped flowers . . . one of the first to invade the bare rock areas." Robert A. Janke, *101 Wildflowers of Isle Royale National Park* (Houghton: Isle Royale Natural History Association/Isle Royale National Park, 1962), 60.

89. "The schooner Algonquin, 50 tons burden, built at Cleveland by Richardson and Mendenhall, was hauled over the portage at Sault Ste. Marie in 1839 and made her first trip on Lake Superior in 1840" (Williams, *The Honorable Peter White*, 112–13). It was the first vessel to be hauled over the portage and "took three and a half months to make that mile-long portage." The *Algonquin* sank near Duluth in 1856. Walter Havighurst, *The Long Ships Passing: The Story of the Great Lakes* (New York: Macmillan, 1942), 163.

90. The *Goliath* (which was also identified as the *Goliah*) blew up on its voyage north across Lake Huron on September 14, 1848, when a fire on board reached dynamite being shipped to the mining region. The *Detroit Free Press* on September 30 based its report on reporting in the *Huron Gazette* in Goderich, Ontario; the *Detroit Daily Advertiser's* report on October 12, 1848, was based on eyewitness accounts in the *Port Huron* (Michigan) *Observer*. The loss of such a vessel could have far-reaching consequences for people dependent upon the supplies shipped to them from the Lower Peninsula. Abner Sherman, who worked in the fur trade on Keweenaw Bay, wrote in a letter dated February 23, 1849, "on arriving at the Sault St M too late to get down after more, I learned that all my goods provisions & groceries had been blown up on the unfortunate Goliah, & I was left to lay out what little means I had left to get back without the necessary provisions to furnish the Indians." Sherman Family Papers, Bentley Historical Library, University of Michigan, Ann Arbor.

91. "John Veale and Lady, Isle Royale," arrived at the Van Anden House on the Michigan with Ruth and C. C. Douglass. He was listed on Ives's survey map as the holder of a location near Ransom, and Mrs. Veale may have been employed by the company.

92. Mr. Shaw's place was the Smithwick Mine, still visible on the outskirts of the present-day Rock Harbor ranger station, lodge, and marina. "In 1848 there were three men there and the shaft was down 90 feet (J[ackson]. pp. 422, 505). By 1849 (J[ackson]., p. 605; F[oster]. and W[hitney]., p. 171) it was down 96 feet. For 30 feet the rock was soft, the vein well developed, expanding in places to 4 feet in width, and containing considerable copper. Then a band of columnar trap was struck and penetrated 66 feet. The vein contracted to a foot in width and was nearly worthless" (Lane, "Part I: Isle Royale," 9).

93. The telegraph had only connected cities in the lower Midwest, such as Chicago and Milwaukee, Detroit and Buffalo, in the earlier part of the year. Communication in the Upper Peninsula still relied on vessels from Sault Ste. Marie or the rarer overland traveler. In the November 1848 elections, Zachary Taylor, the Whig candidate, was elected president, succeeding James K. Polk and defeating the Democratic candidate, General Lewis Cass, former governor of the Michigan Territory. Taylor died in 1850 and was succeeded by his vice-president, Millard Fillmore.

94. The *Detroit Free Press* carried this notice: "DIED—In this City, on the 25th inst., after a lingering and painful illness which she bore with Christian meekness and fortitude, Mrs. Julia C., wife of the Rev. Wm. B. Ashley, and daughter of the late Jesse Hall, of Portland, Connecticut, in the 33d year of her age. Her remains have been taken to her former place of residence in Connecticut, for interment" (October 30, 1848, 2).

95. The proclamation by Governor Epaphroditus Ransom, dated October 30, 1848, and frequently reprinted in the *Detroit Free Press* prior to Thanksgiving, read,

> I do hereby appoint Thursday, the twenty-third day of November next, to be observed as a day of Thanksgiving, Prayer and Praise throughout this State. And I invoke my fellow citizens to abstain, on that day, from their regular employments, and, reparing to their respective places of worship, to render to Almighty God the tribute of thanks so justly due to Him for our bountiful harvests, for the uninterrupted health and prosperity of the people, and for his other rich and varied blessings, munincently [sic] bestowed upon the inhabitants of our favored state and country. (2)

96. George Ehninger of Staten Island arrived at the Van Anden House in Sault Ste. Marie on September 16, 1848, on his way west, and returned there on the *Independence* on October 3, southward bound.

97. Fort Williams was in Thunder Bay, on the Ontario shore. It had started as a fur-trading post of the Northwest Company which, after a bitter rivalry,

merged with the Hudson's Bay Company. By 1848 its fortifications were in disrepair and the decline of the fur trade had diminished its size and importance, although it was still a supply depot and way station for travelers. For people on Isle Royale it was the nearest point of civilization. (See Notes to Introduction, note 101.)

98. The Shaws had three children, a son, C. D. Shaw, and two daughters.

99. Washington Irving published *A History of the Life and Voyages of Christopher Columbus* in four volumes in 1828, then produced an abridged, one-volume version in 1830, the same year he published a sequel, *Voyages and Discoveries of the Companions of Columbus*. In 1848 he published a revised edition, which combined the two works into three volumes, and it may have been this edition that the Douglasses took with them to the island.

100. I have not located the source of this poem, although given the isolation of the Douglasses it would have to be an adaptation of something remembered from an earlier year or an original creation by Ruth Douglass herself.

Epilogue

Ruth and C. C. Douglass left Isle Royale in mid-June, 1849, arriving June 14 at the Ste. Marie Hotel on the propeller *Napoleon.*[1] Without further journals or undiscovered letters it is impossible to account exactly for their movements, but their arrival in Sault Ste. Marie indicates that they were bound for Detroit. There is no record of when they returned to the copper country. From Foster and Whitney's report it seems likely that C. C. remained in the Upper Peninsula. They refer to several sites east of Ontonagon that were explored by C. C. Douglass and John R. Grout, who was also listed with him as one of the directors of the North American Mining Company of Detroit in 1848. The New York and Michigan Company location and the Douglass Houghton Mining Company location were on neighboring sections and both were reported on to their respective companies by Grout and Douglass.[2] More important, Foster and Whitney reported of the Douglass Houghton Mine that in 1847 "the vein was opened to the depth of 40 feet, when further operations were abandoned, but the work has been resumed, under the direction of Mr. C. C. Douglass, one of the most efficient engineers in the region." In their view the "vein is well defined, and affords indications of proving highly valuable." Clearly one of the places where C. C. Douglass could be found in the summer and fall of 1849 was the Douglass Houghton Mine; he had also been retained in 1848 by the Quincy Mine but the work there was temporarily suspended.[3] By 1851, when he left that part of the region to head operations at the revived Quincy Mine on the north shore of Portage Lake, he was working for the Flint and Fire Steel Mining Company, not far from the Douglass Houghton diggings.

The Douglass Houghton, New York and Michigan, Algonquin, and Flint and Fire Steel Mines were inland mines, located in the highlands from which flowed the Flint Steel, Fire Steel, and Ontonagon Rivers. Anton Myers, examining operations in the Ontonagon region in 1851, found it arduous to visit these sites:

> Monday after breakfast were rowed down the lake 7 miles by the Algonquin's men to the Fire steel river, under the direction of George Knox, ascended this beautiful stream 2 miles & lunched at the Storehouse (a little log hut). At an adjoining similiar house, belonging to the Douglas Houghton, were some few pieces of Copper—walked & alternately road 2 mules a distance of 15 execrable miles, which occupied 6 hours. Tuesday morning—viewed this location. . . . From here the Douglas Houghton is 3 miles; we started on the trail directly after an early dinner.[4]

The party was temporarily lost in the thick forest and alarmed by stories of different workers who wandered for days after losing the path. Clearly the locations were difficult of access and Myers wrote of one unnamed site nearby that he did "not think that this Mine can be productive for many years, there must first be a great outlay for roads, exclusive of Engines & other machinery."[5]

By the time of Myers's journey, C. C. Douglass was working at the Quincy Mine, north of Portage Lake. Myers's vessel stopped at Portage Lake to take on wood and Myers went to the store of Ransom Shelden, C. C.'s brother-in-law, where he "received a hospitable welcome & dinner." Either at Shelden's or back on the propeller—the syntax is unclear— "Douglas of the Quincy met me here & detailed circumstantially the condition & prospects of the Mine under his charge. Messrs. Whittlesey & Giddings returned with him to make their report. They had been on Isle Royale to resussitate the Mine previously referred to as abandoned," probably the Ohio and Isle Royale location at Ransom.[6]

In between the period when Foster and Whitney reported C. C. Douglass directing the operations of the Douglass Houghton Mine in 1849 and when Myers reported discussing the Quincy with him in 1851, Ruth Douglass died. The only contemporary account of her death is found in the diary of the Methodist missionary, John Pitezel, dated June 12, 1850:

> Wednesday 12. When I awoke this morning a heavy sea was rolling to the shor too much so to launch the canoe. We held on tite a little befor 5 O Clock & got off. We reached Ontonagon in about half an hour. We were camped about 3 miles off. On arriving I went up to the house of Mr. Beeser & what was my surprise to learn that the wife of Mr. C. C. Douglass was a corps in the house. She was confined a few days ago several miles back in the woods, on a location. Was brought from the

location on a bier in a bed by hand but no help could be obtained—
the summons had come & she must go—she has left her husband & a
little one to feel the deep pangs of human sorrow. How deeply afflict-
ed is Mr. D. May the good Lord in taking away what on earth he
doubtless held dearest, save his soul & bring him to glory.[7]

It is likely that the Douglasses wintered over in the Ontonagon region on a
mining location, probably the Douglass Houghton site. Given the dates of
the child's birth and Ruth's death it is unlikely that she went to Detroit for
the winter and returned to the Upper Peninsula in the spring. She would
have known she was pregnant in the fall and it is probable that by then C.
C. Douglass had a new job—and possibly been working at it—in the
Ontonagon region. Perhaps once again he gave her the option of staying
below rather than wintering over at a mining camp, and perhaps her love
and loyalty and sense of veteran pioneering from her time on Isle Royale
argued in favor of coming north again.

And so she spent another winter in a mining camp, this one as isolated in its own way, by nearly trackless forest and deep winter snows, as
Isle Royale had been. Her son, Edgerton C. Douglass, was born May 27,
1850, and Ruth died June 11, 1850, probably from complications connected with his birth. Even in the best of circumstances, childbirths "were
exhausting and traumatic experiences which weakened mothers for
months; an infected perineal tear or a prolapsed uterus could destroy a
woman's health permanently."[8] In the remote and isolated mining camp, illness and infection were considerly less likely to receive effective treat-
ment. No doubt that was the reason C. C. had his men carry Ruth down
from their location to the settlement of Ontonagon, in hopes of finding
someone who could do something for her. Given Myers's description of the
route he followed to the Douglass Houghton location we can only imagine
how grueling and painful the desperate descent was for Ruth.

Ruth W. Douglass was buried in Elmwood Cemetery in Detroit on
June 20, 1850, after a funeral service in the house of her uncle, Oliver
Newberry, "on Griswold Street, next back of the Baptist Church."[9] In the
1850 census Oliver Newberry's household is listed as including Ruth's
mother, sister, and three-month-old Edgerton C. Douglass. A month and a
half after his mother's death, Edgerton died, on July 29, 1850, and was
buried with his mother. Presumably C. C. Douglass had already gone back
to the copper country. A small white obelisk was erected on the graves of
mother and son, with an inscription for Edgerton on one side and an
inscription for Ruth on another. Her age at her death is given as twenty-five
years, eight months, and twelve days.

For the next decade C. C. Douglass poured his drive and energy into transforming the Portage Lake region. He established a partnership with his brother-in-law Ransom Shelden that was remarkable for both its equality and success. Most accounts of their partnership suggest that it was complementary, the instinct of Shelden balanced by the training of Douglass. In particular, Shelden has been credited for believing in the potential of the Portage Lake region above that of the Keweenaw and the Ontonagon districts and for encouraging Douglass to take charge of the Quincy Mine, which had been moribund. "From mid-March through June of 1851, only a single employee worked at the location, but seventeen were there by the end of July and twenty-eight by late October," when Douglass became superintendent.[10] Shelden established a store near the mine, and the two men began buying considerable areas of land around Portage Lake. Many of the copper mines had played out and only the Quincy, under Douglass, and the Whealkate were working mines, but in 1852 Shelden and Douglass discovered a copper lode south of Portage Lake, the Isle Royale. The mine transferred equipment from the Isle Royale locations of the Ohio and Isle Royale Company and proved highly successful. Together Shelden and Douglass opened the Portage and the Shelden Mines on the same lode in 1853, and over the next several years would open several more, among them the Albion, Douglass, Concord, Arcadian, Columbian, Huron, Dodge, and Jefferson.[11]

But the partners did not only focus on the operations of the mines. Their land investments allowed them to sell locations to other companies, even ones they had not established and did not direct, and Shelden's store was built on the south shore of Portage Lake as a means of supplying the developing district. In the same year that the partners built the store, Shelden platted the village of Houghton with the store as its center and Douglass became "the first individual owner of the land upon which [Hancock] stands, and, in 1852, made his residence thereon, in a log house on the slope of the bluff."[12] The region was growing and becoming more populous and settled, and much of that was due to the enterprise of Shelden and Douglass.

C. C. Douglass married again on September 17, 1856, again in Detroit. His wife was Lydia Reed Smith of Algonac, a village on the St. Clair not far from Mt. Clemens, where his family had settled thirty years earlier. At the time of the wedding C. C. Douglass was forty-four and Lydia was twenty-four.[13] C. C. had moved to Houghton in 1854 and that was where the couple resided. By the time of the 1860 federal census for Houghton County they had a prosperous, settled household. At forty-seven,

Columbus C. Douglass listed himself as a merchant, "Value of Real Estate $175,000, Value of Personal Estate $75,000." In 1861 Columbus became the state representative for Houghton County and moved his family to Lansing, and in 1863 the Douglasses established themselves in New York City, having reversed the westward trend of his family.

Columbus C. Douglass died in London, England, on December 17, 1874, and his death was noted at length in the *Detroit Free Press:*

> He made the Lake Superior region his real residence from 1841 until about ten years since, when he removed to New York. His knowledge of the mineral resources of that portion of our State was very extensive and thorough, and that part of our State owes as much, if not more, to his efforts to make it known and properly appreciated than to any other individual. He had the most unbounded faith in its mineral resources. His visit to England was to promote the sale of large iron interests and to introduce to English iron makers the inexhaustible ore of Lake Superior. He had already induced several extensive manufacturers to visit the lake region to make personal examinations.
>
> Mr. Douglass was simple in his habits, kind in his disposition and lasting in his friendships. His death is not only an irreparable loss to his family and friends, but a great loss to the State. It is understood that his remains will be brought to this city to be interred in Elmwood Cemetery[14]

He was not buried in Elmwood Cemetery but rather in Algonac, under a massive stone engraved with the names of his two daughters who died in infancy, close to Lydia's parents and, eventually, to his son and daughter-in-law and to Lydia and her second husband.[15]

The white obelisk in Elmwood Cemetery, where Ruth and Edgerton rested, weathered in its own space. The Newberrys were buried elsewhere in the cemetery as was C. C.'s uncle Benjamin Douglass and cousin Douglass Houghton. In time small headstones marked the resting places of Ruth's mother, brother, and sister. Fanny was the last to die, in 1894, at seventy-three, nine years after Oliver. She provided for a monument to the Edgerton family, commemorating on one side Isaac, Louisa, and herself, and on the other two infant nephews, Edgerton and Franklin, Oliver's son, as well as Oliver and Ruth. A stone figure of a sitting woman adorns the top of the memorial.

For over a hundred years that stone and the obelisk beside it, the inscription of which is slowly disappearing, have served as the only memorial of the brief life of Ruth Edgerton Douglass. When her journal was sold to the Clarke Library nearly one hundred and forty years after it was written, a list of Lydia Douglass's siblings inserted in its pages misled catalogers to believe that it was the journal of the second Mrs. C. C. Douglass. Ruth Edgerton Douglass, who had a wry and resilient sense of humor, would appreciate the restoration of this holograph memorial as ironic evidence of the way that "time by moments steals away."

Notes

1. *Lake Superior Journal,* June 15, 1849.
2. Foster and Whitney, *Report on the Geology and Topography* . . . , 67, 71–72.
3. Ibid., 142, 150–51.
4. A. Myers, Transcript of Journey to Siskowit Mine in 1851, Historical Society of Pennsylvania, Philadelphia. AM 448 Myers, July 29 and 30.
5. Ibid., July 30, 1851.
6. Ibid., August 19, 1851. The Whittlesey here is probably Colonel Charles Whittlesey, a cousin of the Whittlesey who ran the Siskowit Mine. He drafted several reports to Giddings later in the 1851 season from Eagle River. In one he opined that "Mr. Douglass has adopted the most effacacious mode of exploration; by digging a trench, around [illegible] of the hill, across the general course of the veins." A later report (1854) has notes attached, which refer to "Extracts from C. C. Douglass letters to C. M. Gidings [*sic*] relating to Quincy Mines on Portage Lake" and are dated as early as December 13, 1850. Charles Whittlesey Papers, Western Reserve Historical Library, Cleveland.

    Whittlesey also spoke highly of C. C. Douglass's abilities: "Mr. Douglass was also engaged upon the Government Survey of that country; he has spent seven years there, as superintendent of mines and from his intelligence as a practical geologist and miner I do not hesitate to adopt his statement as my own." Charles Whittlesey, "Report of Charles Whittlesey, Agent, to the President and Directors, Siskowit Mining Company, May 25, 1848," *American Mining Journal and Rail Road Gazette* (June 21, 1848): 5.
7. John H. Pitezel, Journal entry dated June 12, 1850, John H. Pitezel Papers, Clarke Historical Library, Central Michigan University, Mt. Pleasant. When Pitezel published a book about his missionary life in the Upper Peninsula, drawn heavily from his journals, he dropped the final two sentences. Spending the night in a public house next door to that of Martin Beaser, who ran a store in Ontonagon, Pitezel was outraged at the uproar of drunken men—"drinking, swearing, dancing, and singing, all in perfect tumult"— especially because "the deceased wife of Mr. D" was lying next door. His concern in both works primarily seems to be the effects of alcohol on men (*Lights and Shades of Missionary Life,* 257–58).
8. Jack Larkin, *The Reshaping of Everyday Life,* 1790–1840 (New York: Harper and Row, 1988), 95.
9. *Detroit Free Press,* June 20, 1850, 2.
10. Larry Lankton, *Cradle to Grave: Life, Work, and Death at the Lake Superior Copper Mines* (New York: Oxford University Press, 1991), 7.

11. James Russell and Albert Hornstein, *First Annual Review of the Copper Mining Industry of Lake Superior* (Marquette, Mich.: Mining Journal Co., Ltd., 1899), 33.

12. *History of the Upper Peninsula of Michigan*, 287. Their enterprises further expanded when Douglass became the first supervisor of the new township of Portage, encompassing most of what is now Houghton County, in 1853, "the whole number of votes cast being 28 [and] no opposition." He was re-elected the following year with opposition. Graham Pope, "Some Early Mining Days at Portage Lake," *Proceedings of the Lake Superior Mining Institute* (Houghton: Lake Superior Mining Institute, 1901), 7:23.

    In 1855 he bought a small stern-wheel steamer, remodeled it for a side-wheeler, and named it the *C. C. Douglass*. It was the first commercial vessel on Portage Lake and neighboring Torch Lake to run passengers and supplies inland to Hancock and Houghton from Portage Entry (*History of the Upper Peninsula*, 254). Later Shelden and Douglass would go into partnership with the mining companies to dredge the entry into the lake and make it deep enough for lake vessels to enter, vastly improving the ability to ship ore from the mines (Pope, "Some Early Mining Days," 27). In 1856 Douglass was appointed postmaster of Houghton: "The office was kept in the store of R. Shelden & Co. (C. C. Douglass being the 'Co.'). Mr. Douglass was succeeded by Edward F. Douglass (a cousin), August 27, 1861, he being the first Republican postmaster" (*History of the Upper Peninsula*, 274).

13. In 1860 C. C. Douglass's household included his wife, Lydia, 26, his three-month-old daughter, Jennie, two of his wife's sisters, Anna Smith, 31, and Kate, 23, her brother, S. Latta Smith, 28, and two servants, Margaret Campbell, 20, and Bridgett Healey, 16. Ransom Shelden, who lived in the very next building, was worth an identical sum of real and personal estate, since the partners shared everything equally. Shelden lived with his wife, three sons, a daughter, a schoolteacher, two female relatives, and a servant originally from Canada. *Houghton County Federal Census, 1860* (Lansing: State of Michigan, Central Microfilm Services, 1984).

14. *Detroit Free Press*, December 20, 1874, 1.

15. C. C. and Lydia's first child, Jessie H. Douglass, was born November 14, 1857, but lived only three months. Jennie P. Douglass died at the age of eight months, thirteen days, on a visit to grandparents in Algonac. Their son, Courtney C. Douglass, was born in Algonac in 1862. In later years Courtney returned to Houghton to manage his father's business affairs. Courtney died in Houghton in 1924, and he and his wife, Helen Bardwell Douglass, who died in 1945, are buried in Algonac. C. C. and Lydia's fourth child was Katharine, who married Nathan Y. Worrall and lived in Philadelphia. Lydia, twenty years younger than Columbus, remarried and is buried with her second husband, Elizur Hinsdale, in the cemetery in Algonac. She died in 1912.

Appendix A

Douglass Family Genealogy

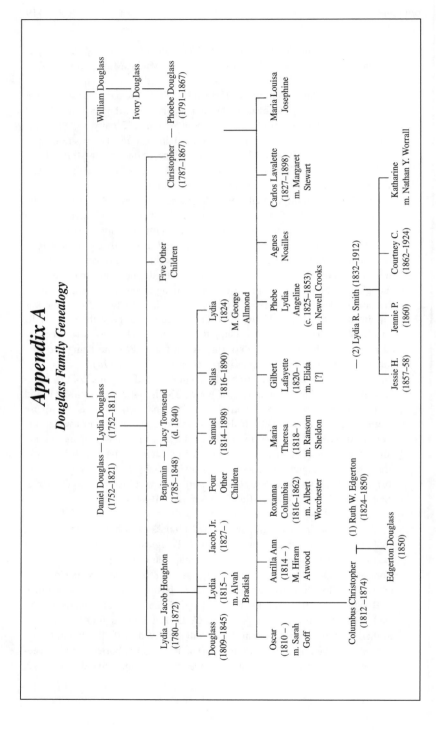

Appendix B
Newberry Family Genealogy

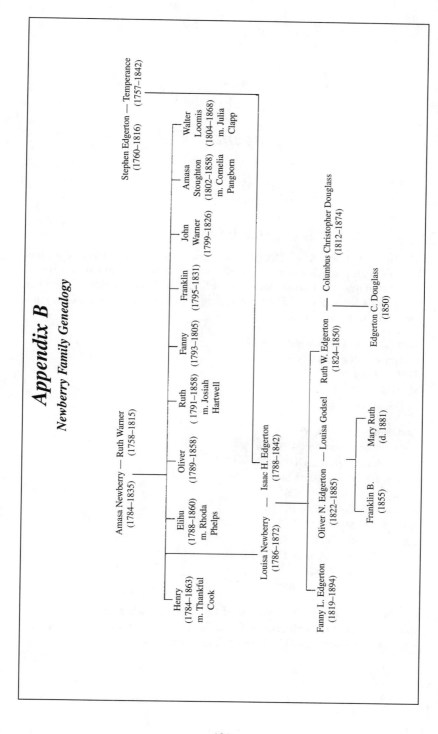

Appendix C

Smith Family

The Journal of Mrs. C. C. Douglass was purchased by the Clarke Historical Library with a single sheet of paper inserted. It was a handwritten list of the birthdates of family members of Lydia Reed Smith, Columbus Douglass's second wife. The handwriting is different from that of the journal itself. It reads as follows:

John K. Smith Tuesday Nov. 29th 1785
Catharine McDonald Glasgow, Scotland
31st October 1795
Married
2nd December 1818

Abraham Smith Sept. 8th 1819
Sarah Smith December 24th 1820.
Angus Smith December 16th 1822.
Jane Smith October 3rd 1824.
Anna Smith April 25th 1826.
Samuel latta Smith June 28th 1830.
Lydia Smith May 9th 1832.
Catharine Smith June 5th 1834.
Mary & Frances February 11th 1836.
Mary died Sep. 7th 1836.
Mary Smith March 18th 1838.

Anna Smith was the executor of C. C. Douglass's estate, and received a third of it. In the 1860 census Anna, Catharine, and Latta Smith were living in the household of C. C. and Lydia in Houghton.

Bibliography

Manuscripts and Archival Materials

Douglass, C. C. Letter to Abram Sager, November 19, 1841. Abram Sager Papers. Bentley Historical Library. Ann Arbor, Michigan.

Douglass, C. C. Letter to Mr. C[hristopher] Douglass, June 23, 1844. Douglas Worrall Collection. State Archives of Michigan, Lansing.

Douglass, C. C. Letter to Ransom Shelden, November 20, 1847. Roy Drier Collection. Michigan Technological University Archives. Houghton.

Douglass Papers. Bentley Historical Library. University of Michigan, Ann Arbor.

Helen, Letter, 1847. Clarke Historical Library. Central Michigan University, Mt. Pleasant.

Houghton, Jacob. Papers. Bentley Historical Library. University of Michigan, Ann Arbor.

Hubbard, Bela. Papers. Bentley Historical Library. University of Michigan, Ann Arbor.

Journal of a Trip to Michigan, 1848. MSS JJ-75. Clarke Historical Library. Central Michigan University, Mt. Pleasant.

Myers, A. Transcript of Journey to Siskowit Mine in 1851. Historical Society of Pennsylvania, Philadelphia. AM 448 12 pp. (July 8–August 31, 1851).

Pitezel, John H. Papers, 1828–1889. Clarke Historical Library. Central Michigan University, Mt. Pleasant.

Ransom, Leander. Letter to Elisha Whittlesey, January 6, 1847. Elisha Whittlesey Papers. Western Reserve Historical Society. Cleveland.

Shaw, Cornelius. Diary (1847). Bentley Historical Library. University of Michigan, Ann Arbor.

Whittlesley, Charles. Papers. Western Reserve Historical Library. Cleveland.

Whittlesley, Elisha. Papers. Western Reserve Historical Library. Cleveland.

Mining and Geological Reports

Cassels, J. Lang. *Geological and Mineralogical Report upon the Mineral Lands on Isle Royale, Lake Superior, Belonging to the Isle Royale & Ohio Mining Company.* Cleveland: Smead and Cowles, 1846.

Charter and By-Laws of the Siskowit Mining Company of Michigan, together with the Treasurer's Report, &c. up to January 1, 1850. Philadelphia: John Clarke, 1850.

Foster, J. W., and J. D. Whitney. *Report on the Geology and Topography of the Lake Superior Land District in the State of Michigan. Part I. Copperlands.* Washington: Printed for the House of Representatives, 1850–51.

Houghton, Jacob, Jr. *The Mineral Regions of Lake Superior.* Buffalo: O. Steele, 1846.

Houghton, Jacob, Jr., and T. W. Bristol. *Reports of William A. Burt and Bela Hubbard, esqs., on the Geography, Topography, and Geology of the U.S. Surveys of the Mineral Region of the South Shore of Lake Superior for 1845.* Detroit: Charles Willcox, 1846.

Isle Royale and Ohio Mining Co. *Articles of Association of the Isle Royale and Ohio Mining Company, with a Description of Their Property.* Cincinnati: L'Hommedieu and Co., 1846.

Jackson, Charles T. *Report to the Trustees of Lake Superior Copper Company.* Boston: Beals and Greene, 1845.

Lane, Alfred C. "Part I: Isle Royale." In *The Upper Peninsula, 1893–1897, Volume 6.* Lansing: Robert Smith Printing, 1898.

Senate. *Report on the Geological and Mineralogical Survey of the Mineral Lands of the United States in the State of Michigan,* by Charles T. Jackson. 31st Cong., 1st sess., 1849–50, S. Doc. 1, pt. 3.

Swineford, A. P. *History and Review of the Copper, Iron, Silver, Slate, and Other Material Interests of the South Shore of Lake Superior.* Marquette: Mining Journal, 1876.

Whittlesey, Charles. *Ancient Mining on the Shores of Lake Superior.* Smithsonian Contributions to Knowledge 155. Washington, D.C.: Smithsonian Institution, 1863.

Books and Articles

Adams, Charles C. *An Ecological Survey of Isle Royale, Lake Superior.* Lansing: Wynkoop Hallenbeck Crawford, 1909.

American Biographical History of Eminent and Self-Made Men: Michigan Volume. Cincinnati: Western Biographical Publishing, 1878.

Andreas, A. T. *History of Chicago from the Earliest Period to the Present Time.* 3 vols. Chicago: A. T. Andreas, 1884.

Bartlett, Joseph Gardner. *Newberry Genealogy: The Ancestors and Descendents of Thomas Newberry of Dorchester, Mas, 1634–1914.* Boston: J. G. Bartlett, 1914.

Bayliss, Joseph E., and Estelle L. Bayliss, in collaboration with Milo Quaife. *River of Destiny: The Saint Marys.* Detroit: Wayne State University Press, 1955.

Beckwith, Albert Clayton. *History of Walworth County, Wisconsin.* 2 vols. Indianapolis: B. F. Bowen and Co., 1912.

Biographical Record of Houghton, Baraga, and Marquette Counties. Chicago: Biographical Publishing Co., 1903.

Bradish, Alvah. *Memoir of Douglass Houghton, First State Geologist of Michigan.* Detroit: Raynor and Taylor, 1889.

Bremer, Fredrika. *The Homes of the New World: Impressions of America.* Trans. Mary Howitt. 2 vols. 1853. Reprint, New York: Johnson Reprint Corporation, 1968.

Bryant, William Cullen. *The Letters of William Cullen Bryant, 1836–1849.* 3 vols. Ed. William Cullen Bryant II and Thomas G. Voss. New York: Fordham University Press, 1977.

Catlin, George B. *A Brief History of Detroit in the Golden Days of '49.* Detroit: Detroit Savings Bank, 1921.

———. "Oliver Newberry." *Michigan History* 18 (winter 1934): 5–24.

———. *The Story of Detroit.* Detroit: Detroit News, 1923.

Chase, Lew Allen. "Early Copper Mining in Michigan." *Michigan History* 29:1 (January–March 1945): 22–30.

———. "Michigan Copper Mines," *Michigan History* 29:4 (October–December 1945): 479–88.

Clarke, Don H. *The United States Mineral Agency.* The Copper Mines of Keweenaw 1. N.p., 1973.

Clarke, Robert E. "Notes from the Copper Region." *Harper's New Monthly Magazine* 6, no. 34 (March 1853): 433–49; 6, no. 35 (April 1853): 577–88.

Combination Atlas Map of Walworth County, Wisconsin. Chicago: Everts, Baskin, and Stewart, 1873.

Daily Advertiser Directory for the City of Detroit for the Year 1850. Detroit: Duncklee, Wales, and Co., 1850.

Disturnell, John. *A Trip Through the Lakes of North America.* New York: J. Disturnell, 1857.

Dobrée, Bonamy. Introduction to *The Bachelor of the Albany [by Marmion W. Savage].* New York: Frederic A. Stokes, 1928.

Douglas, J. Lufkin. *The Douglas Genealogy.* Bath, Me.: Sentinel and Times Publishing, 1890.

Dunlop, M. H. *Sixty Miles from Contentment: Traveling the Nineteenth-Century American Interior.* New York: Basic Books, 1995.

Dustin, Fred. *An Archaeological Reconnaisance of Isle Royale.* Lansing: Michigan Historical Commission, 1957.

———."Isle Royale Place Names." *Michigan History* 30, no. 4 (October–December 1946): 681–722.

Eldridge, Robert F. *Past and Present of Macomb County.* Chicago: Clarke Publishing, 1905.

Fadner, Lawrence T. *Fort Wilkins, 1844, and the U.S. Mineral Agency, 1843, Copper Harbor, Michigan, Lake Superior.* New York: Vantage Press, 1966.

Farmer, Silas. *The History of Detroit and Michigan, or The Metropolis Illustrated: A Chronological Cyclopaedia of the Past and Present.* Detroit: Silas Farmer and Co., 1884.

Forster, John Harris. "Early Settlement of the Copper Regions of Lake Superior," *Pioneer Collections: Report of the Pioneer Society of the State of Michigan.* Vol. 7. Lansing: Thorp and Godfrey, 1884.

————. "Lake Superior Country." *Pioneer Collections: Report of the Pioneer Society of the State of Michigan*. Vol. 8. Lansing: Wynkoop, Hallenbeck, Crawford Co., 1885.

————. "Some Incidents of Pioneer Life in the Upper Peninsula of Michigan," *Pioneer Collections: Report of the Pioneer Society of the State of Michigan*. Vol. 17. Lansing: Wynkoop, Hallenbeck, Crawford Co., 1892.

Gazetteer of the State of Michigan. Detroit: S. L. Rood, 1838.

Geddes, Irene. *Index of Names in History of Macomb, County, Michigan*. Mount Clemens, Mich.: Macomb County Genealogy Group, 1986.

Gilchrist, Marie E. "Isle Royale Survey, Part I." *Inland Seas* 24, no. 3 (fall 1968): 179–92.

————. "Isle Royale Survey, Part II." *Inland Seas* 24, no. 4 (winter 1968): 303–25.

————. "Isle Royale Survey, Part III," *Inland Seas* 25, no. 1 (spring 1969): 26–40.

Greeley, Horace. "Lake Superior—Copper Mining—The 'Cliff'." *American Mining Journal and Railroad Gazette* 2 (1848/1849): 58.

————. *Recollections of a Busy Life*. New York: J. B. Ford and Co., 1868.

Havighurst, Walter. *The Long Ships Passing: The Story of the Great Lakes*. New York: Macmillan, 1942.

Heyl, Erik. *Early American Steamers*. 6 vols. Buffalo: N.p., 1953–1969.

"Historical Sketch of the Lake Superior Copper District." In *The 1924 Keweenawan*, 217–88. Houghton: Michigan College of Mines, 1924.

History of Macomb County, Michigan. Chicago: M. A. Lesson, 1882.

History of St. Clair County, Michigan. Chicago: A. T. Andreas, 1883.

History of the Upper Peninsula of Michigan. Chicago: Western Historical, 1883.

History of Walworth County, Wisconsin. Chicago: Western Historical Co., 1882.

Hood, Thomas. *Up the Rhine*. 2nd ed. Philadelphia: Porter and Coates, 1840.

Houghton, Douglass. *Geological Reports of Douglass Houghton, First State Geologist of Michigan, 1837–1845*. Ed. George N. Fuller. Lansing: Michigan Historical Commission, 1928.

Houghton County Federal Census, 1860. Lansing: State of Michigan, Central Microfilm Services, 1984.

Houghton County Federal Census, 1864. Lansing: State of Michigan, Central Microfilm Services, 1984.

Hubbard, Bela. *Lake Superior Journal: Bela Hubbard's Account of the 1840 Houghton Expedition*. Ed. Bernard C. Peters. Marquette, Mich.: Northern Michigan University Press, 1983.

————. *Memorials of a Half-century in Michigan and the Lake Region*. New York: G. P. Putnam's Sons, 1888.

————. "A Michigan Geological Expedition in 1837." *Pioneer Collections: Report of the Pioneer Society of the State of Michigan*. Vol. 3. Lansing: W. S. George and Co., 1881.

Hunt, John Warren. *The Wisconsin Gazetteer*. Madison: B. Brown, 1853.

Hybels, Robert James. "The Lake Superior Copper Fever, 1841–1847." *Michigan History* 34, no. 2 (June 1950): 97–119; 34, no. 3 (September 1950): 224–44; 34, no. 4 (December 1950): 309–27.

Janke, Robert A. *101 Wildflowers of Isle Royale National Park.* Houghton: Isle Royale Natural History Association/Isle Royale National Park, 1962.

Jeffrey, Julie Roy. *Frontier Women: The Trans-Mississippi West, 1840–1880.* New York: Hill and Wang, 1979.

Jenks, William Lee. *St. Clair County, Michigan: Its History and Its People.* New York: Lewis Publishing Co., 1912.

Karamanski, Theodore J., and Richard Zeitlin. *Narrative History of Isle Royale National Park.* Chicago: Mid-American Research Center, Loyola University of Chicago, 1988.

Kirkland, Caroline. *Western Clearings.* New York: Putnam, 1845.

Krause, David J. *The Making of a Mining District: Keweenaw Native Copper 1500–1870.* Detroit: Wayne State University Press, 1992.

Lankton, Larry. *Cradle to Grave: Life, Work, and Death at the Lake Superior Copper Mines.* New York: Oxford University Press, 1991.

Lankton, Larry D., and Charles K. Hyde. *Old Reliable: An Illustrated History of the Quincy Mining Company.* Hancock, Mich.: Quincy Mine Hoist Association, 1982.

Lanman, Charles. *A Summer in the Wilderness Embracing a Canoe Voyage up the Mississippi and around Lake Superior.* New York: D. Appleton and Company, 1847.

Larkin, Jack. *The Reshaping of Everyday Life, 1790–1840.* New York: Harper and Row, 1988.

Lee, Helen Bourne Joy. *The Newberry Genealogy.* Chester, Conn.: Pequot Press, 1975.

Lenormand, Marie Anne. *Historical and Secret Memoirs of the Empress Josephine.* Trans. Jacob M. Howard. 2 vols. Philadephia: John E. Potter, n.d.

MacCabe, Julius P. Bolivar. *Directory of the City of Detroit with Its Environs and Register of Michigan, for the Year 1837.* Detroit: William Harsha, 1837.

McLeod, Donald. *History of Wiskonsan, From Its First Discovery to the Present Period.* Buffalo: Steele's Press, 1846.

Marriage Records from Archives of Wayne County, Michigan. 12 vols. Lansing: Michigan State Library/Daughters of the American Revolution Louisa St. Clair Chapter, 1936.

Marriages 1827–1857 in Washtenaw County, Michigan. Lansing: Michigan State Library, 1961.

Martineau, Harriet. *Society in America.* 3 vols. London: Saunders and Otley, 1837. Reprint, New York: AMS Press, 1966.

Marvill, Lewis. "First Trip by Steam to Lake Superior." *Pioneer Collections: Report of the Pioneer Society of the State of Michigan.* Vol. 4. Lansing: W. S. George and Co., 1883.

Memorial Record of the Northern Peninsula of Michigan. Chicago: Lewis Publishing Co., 1895.

Michigan Biographies. 2 vols. Lansing: Michigan Historical Commission, 1924.

Moynihan, Ruth B., Susan Armitage, and Christiane Fischer Dichamp, eds. *Much to Be Done: Women Settlers on the Mining and Ranching Frontier.* Lincoln: University of Nebraska Press, 1990.

Murdoch, Angus. *Boom Copper: The Story of the First U.S. Mining Boom.* 1943. Reprint, Hancock, Mich.: Drier and Koepel, 1964.

Nichols, Roger L. "Black Hawk (Makataimeshekiakiak)." In *Encyclopedia of North American Indians*, ed. Frederick E. Hoxie, 76–78. Boston: Houghton Mifflin, 1996.

Palmer, Friend. *Early Days in Detroit.* Detroit: Hunt and Jones, 1906.

Parkins, Almon Ernest. *The Historical Geography of Detroit.* 1918. Reprint, Port Washington, N.Y.: Kennikat Press, 1970.

Partridge, Charles Addison. *Lake County.* Chicago: Munsell Publishing, 1902.

Penny, Charles W. *North to Lake Superior: The Journal of Charles W. Penny, 1840.* Ed. James L. Carter and Ernest H. Rankin. Sesquicentennial Edition. Marquette, Mich.: John M. Longyear Research Library, 1987.

Pierce, Bessie L. *A History of Chicago.* 2 vols. New York: Knopf, 1937.

Pitezel, John H. *Lights and Shades of Missionary Life.* Cincinnati: Western Book Concern, 1857.

Pope, Graham. "Some Early Mining Days at Portage Lake." *Proceedings of the Lake Superior Mining Institute.* Vol. 7. Houghton: Lake Superior Mining Institute, 1901.

Portrait and Biographical Record of Walworth and Huron Counties, Wisconsin. Chicago: Lake Publishing, 1894.

Pyne, William H. "Quincy Mine: The Old Reliable." *Michigan History* 41, no. 2 (June 1957): 219–42.

Quaife, Milo M. *Chicago's Highways, Old and New, From Indian Trail to Motor Road.* Chicago: D. F. Keller and Co., 1923.

Rakestraw, Lawrence Frederick. *Historic Mining on Isle Royale.* Houghton: Isle Royale Natural History Association in cooperation with the National Park Service, 1965.

"Recollections of an Old Copper Country Resident," *The Calumet News,* March 17, 1913: 4.

Rintala, Edsel K. *Douglass Houghton, Michigan's Pioneer Geologist.* Detroit: Wayne University Press, 1954.

[Rundel, Andrew.] "A Copper Prospector in 1846." Ed. Alice E. Smith. *Michigan History* 33, no. 2 (June 1949): 141–54.

Russell, James, and Albert Hornstein. *First Annual Review of the Copper Mining Industry of Lake Superior.* Marquette, Mich.: Mining Journal Co., Ltd., 1899.

St. John, John. *A True Description of the Lake Superior Country.* New York: William H. Graham, 1846. Reprint, Grand Rapids: Black Letter Press, 1976.

Savage, Marmion W. *The Bachelor of the Albany.* New York: Harper and Brothers, 1848.

Sawyer, Alvah L. *History of the Northern Peninsula of Michigan and Its Peoples.* 3 vols. Chicago: Lewis Publishing, 1911.

Shelton, Napier. *The Life of Isle Royale.* Washington: Office of Publications, National Park Service, 1975.

Shove's Business Advertiser and Detroit Directory for 1852–53. Detroit: Free Press Book and Job Office Printing, 1852.

Smith, J. Calvin. *The Western Tourist or Emigrant's Guide.* New York: John Colton, 1845.

————. *The Western Tourist or Emigrant's Guide.* New York: John Colton, 1847.

Stonehouse, Frederick. *Great Wrecks of the Great Lakes.* Marquette, Mich.: Harboridge Press, 1973.

Swayze, David D. *Shipwreck! A Comprehensive Directory of Over 3,700 Shipwrecks on the Great Lakes.* Boyne City, Mich.: Harbor House, 1992.

Van Dorn, Luther. "A View of Chicago in 1848." *Magazine of Western History* 10, no. 1 (May 1889): 41–46.

Vital Records of Norwich, Connecticut, 1659–1848. Hartford, Conn.: Society of Colonial Wars in the State of Connecticut, 1913.

Vital Records from the Detroit Free Press. [Detroit]: Michigan State Library/Daughters of the American Revolution, 1939.

Waggoner, Clark. *History of the City of Toledo and Lucas County, Ohio.* New York: Munsell and Company, 1888.

Wellings, James H. *Directory of the City of Detroit and Register of Michigan for the Year 1845.* Detroit: Harsha and Willcox, 1845.

————. *Directory of the City of Detroit and Register of Michigan for the Year 1846.* Detroit: A. S. Williams, 1846.

Whittlesey, Charles. "Report of Charles Whittlesey, Agent, to the President and Directors, Siskowit Mining Company, May 25, 1848." *American Mining Journal and Rail Road Gazette,* June 21, 1848.

————. "Two Months in the Copper Region." In *Fugitive Essays,* 282–344. Hudson, Ohio: Sawyer, Ingersoll, and Co., 1852.

Wickham, Gertrude Van Rensselaer. *The Pioneer Families of Cleveland, 1796–1840.* 2 vols. Cleveland: Cleveland Centennial Commission, 1914.

Williams, Ralph D. *The Honorable Peter White.* Cleveland: Penton Publishing Co., 1907.

Wolf, Julius F., Jr. *Julius F. Wolf, Jr.'s Lake Superior Shipwrecks.* 2nd ed. Duluth: Lake Superior Port Cities, 1990.

Index

Apostle Islands, 108n. 76. *See also* La
    Pointe, Wisconsin
Atwood, Aurilla Douglass, 22, 63, 92n.
    3, 93n. 10

Bremer, Fredrika, 27; on Chicago, 32;
    on Detroit, 27; on Milwaukee, 32;
    on travel by railroad, 30; on travel
    by stagecoach, 30–31, 33–34; on
    Wisconsin, 33–34
Bryant, William Cullen: on Chicago,
    31–32; on Mackinac Island, 35; on
    Milwaukee, 32; on Sault Ste.
    Marie, 36

Clarke Historical Library (Mt.
    Pleasant, Mich.), 15, 117
Chicago, 30, 31, 55, 61–62, 100n. 36

Detroit, 25–29, 63–65; great fire in,
    63, 101n. 41; illness in, 58
Douglass, Benjamin, 64, 103n. 51
Douglass, Carlos Lavalette, 25, 57,
    93n. 10
Douglass, Christopher, 21, 22, 25, 33,
    47n. 8, 58–59, 91n. 2, 93n. 10
Douglass, Columbus C. (C. C.), 15, 16,
    17, 20, 22–25, 27, 28, 29, 30, 31,
    48n. 9, 52n. 92. 53, 54, 56, 57, 58,
    60, 64, 91n. 2; death of, 117; on
    Isle Royale, 37, 43, 44, 68–91
Douglass, Edgerton C., 115, 117

Douglass, Josephine, 55, 56, 59, 93n.
    10
Douglass, Lydia Reed Smith, 116–17,
    119nn. 13, 15
Douglass, Ruth: birth of, 15; death of,
    15, 114–15, 117–18; in Chicago,
    32, 61–62; in Detroit, 18–19,
    26–29, 53–54, 63–65; in Sault Ste.
    Marie, 37, 66, 113; in Walworth,
    Wisconsin, 19, 29–30, 32–34,
    54–61; journalkeeping of, 15, 16;
    marriage to C. C. Douglass, 25; on
    Isle Royale, 16–21, 37, 41, 44, 45,
    46, 52n. 92. 68–91; on Mackinac
    Island, 37, 65
Douglass, Samuel T., 22, 47n. 8, 54,
    92n. 3
Douglass, Silas H., 22, 47n. 8, 93n. 10
Douglass family, 47n. 8, 55–61, 93n.
    10, 103n. 51, 120
Douglass Houghton Mining Company,
    24, 113–14, 115
Dunlop, M. H.: on land speculation, 21

Edgerton, Fanny Louisa, 21–22, 29,
    57, 63, 64, 81, 85, 117
Edgerton, Isaac Huntington, 15, 21,
    29, 47n. 7, 117
Edgerton, Louisa Newberry, 15,
    21–22, 29, 46n. 7, 64, 81, 117
Edgerton, Oliver Newberry, 21–22, 25,
    28–29, 31, 32, 46n. 7, 62, 65, 100n.
    37, 102n. 50, 107n. 74, 115

Edgerton, Ruth Warner. *See* Ruth Douglass
Elmwood Cemetery, Detroit, 15, 64, 115, 117

Forster, John Harris, 25, 49n. 20
Foster and Whitney: report by, 43, 44, 113

Giddings, Charles Mattoon, 45, 65, 73, 74, 75–76, 81, 104n. 54, 114, 118n. 6
Goliath: sinking of the, 45, 75, 110n. 90
Greeley, Horace, 40–41, 66, 107nn. 72, 75

"Helen": on Detroit, 26
Houghton, Douglass, 22–24, 27, 37, 45, 47n. 8, 48n. 9
Houghton, Jacob, Jr., 22, 24, 47n. 8, 48n. 9
Hubbard, Bela, 22–23, 48n. 10, 60, 96n. 26
Hubbard, James, 71, 76, 78, 83, 87, 88

Isle Royale, 15, 16, 17, 37–46, 51–53, 65–91
Isle Royale & Ohio Mining Company, 16, 38, 39–40, 41, 42, 43, 45, 103n. 53

Jackson, Dr. Charles T., 24, 38, 41, 45
Jeffrey, Julie Roy, 20

Keweenaw Peninsula, 37, 40–41, 116–17
Kirkland, Caroline, 31
Koch, C. L.: visit to Isle Royale, 42

La Pointe, Wisconsin, 66, 76, 81, 107n. 73
Lake Michigan: storm on, 61–62, 98n. 32
Lake Superior Mining Company, 24–25, 107n. 75

Lanman, Charles: on Lake Superior, 44; on Mackinac Island, 35; on Sault Ste. Marie, 36

Mackinac Island, 35–36, 37, 65, 105n. 63
Macomb County, Michigan, 21, 22, 59, 91n. 2
Manitou Islands, 34–35, 100n. 34
Martineau, Harriet, 27, 31, 95n. 16; on Chicago, 31; on Michigan, 92nn. 6, 7; on stagecoaches, 30; on Wisconsin, 33, 34
Masters, Jane: at Siskowit Mine, 52n. 92
Matthews, Mark, 21, 70, 72, 76, 109n. 80
Matthews, Mrs. [Mark], 18, 21, 73, 74, 76
McCulloch, H. H., 42, 43, 71, 72–73, 74, 75, 78, 84, 110n. 86
Michigan Geological Survey, 22–23, 37–38, 49
Milwaukee, 32, 62, 101n. 40
Mott, Angelique, and Charlie: on Isle Royale, 52n. 92, 69, 108n. 79
Myers, Anton: visit to Upper Peninsula, 42–43, 45–46, 114

Newberry, Elihu, 22, 47n. 7
Newberry, Henry, 22, 28, 47n. 7, 100n. 37
Newberry, Louisa. *See* Louisa Newberry Edgerton
Newberry, Oliver, 22, 25, 28–29, 31, 32, 47n. 7, 62, 84, 100n. 37, 102n. 50, 107n. 74, 115
Newberry, Walter Loomis, 31, 62, 100n. 38
Newberry family, 15, 21, 46n. 7, 121

Ohio & Isle Royale Mining Company. *See* Isle Royale & Ohio Mining Company
Ontonagon, Michigan, 15, 108n. 78, 113–15

Palmer, General Friend, 27
Pitezel, Rev. John: on Ruth Douglass's death, 114–15, 118n. 7
Pittsburg and Isle Royale Mining Company, 42, 43

Rakestraw, Lawrence: on Isle Royale mining, 42

Sangerfield, New York, 15, 21
Sault Ste. Marie, 35, 36, 37, 66, 81, 105nn. 66, 67, 113
Shaw, Cornelius, 20–21, 42, 43, 45, 70, 71, 77, 78, 83, 84, 87, 88, 109n. 83, 112n. 98
Shelden, Ransom, 25, 27, 94n. 11, 114, 116, 119nn. 12, 13
Siskowit Mine, 19, 39, 42, 43, 45, 52n. 92, 69, 87, 108n. 79
Smith family, 122

Smithwick Mine, 42, 43, 109n. 83, 111n. 92

Telegraph, 28, 69, 80, 111n. 93
Travel: by lake vessel, 26, 28–29, 30, 32, 34, 60–62, 97n. 30, 103n. 52, 106n. 69; by railroad, 26, 28, 30, 92n. 5; by stagecoach, 28, 30, 55, 60, 61

Veale, Mrs. [John], 77, 79, 111n. 91

Walworth, Wisconsin, 21, 24, 29–30, 33–34, 55–60, 92n. 4
Whittlesey, Charles, 39, 42, 87, 114
Wisconsin, 30, 32–34, 55–61, 92n. 4, 93n. 9, 94nn. 12, 13, 95nn. 14, 15, 18, 96n. 21